CW00502712

GO NAKED:
THE CREDIBLE EXPERT

How to Stand Out in Medical Sales, Create More Opportunities, and Grow Your Business

MICHAEL SMITH

DARK RIVER

Published in 2016 by Dark River, an imprint of Bennion Kearny Limited.

Copyright © Michael Smith

GO NAKED® is a Registered Trademark of Developed Edge Ltd.

ISBN: 978-1-911121-20-6

All Rights Reserved. No part of this publication may be reproduced, stored in a retrieval system, or transmitted in any form or by any means, electronic, mechanical, photocopying, recording or otherwise, without the prior permission of the publisher.

This book is sold subject to the condition that it shall not, by way of trade or otherwise, be lent, re-sold, hired out or otherwise circulated without the publisher's prior consent in any form of binding or cover other than that it which it is published and without a similar condition including this condition being imposed on the subsequent purchaser.

Dark River has endeavoured to provide trademark information about all the companies and products mentioned in this book by the appropriate use of capitals. However, Dark River cannot guarantee the accuracy of this information.

Published by Dark River, an imprint of Bennion Kearny Limited
6 Woodside
Churnet View Road
Oakamoor
ST10 3AE

ACKNOWLEDGEMENTS

A friend of mine wrote me an email recently. In it he said, 'how did you find the time to write another book?' The answer of course is that I made a choice. I decided to do it. Got started. Held myself to account and involved the right people.

That last step however is *the* defining step.

Involving the right people.

I am incredibly fortunate to have many wonderful, generous and supportive people around me and I'd like to take a moment to acknowledge them. Without them, this project wouldn't have gotten started and wouldn't have been completed.

The open, inclusive and trusting people who gave us our early opportunities when we set out with just a philosophy and an idea. John Aiken, Carl Riley, Jon Dawson, Tony and Robert Keily, and Mark Oldroyd.

The supportive people who have provided help in wide ranging ways. Andy Gilbert, Darren Garwood, Michelle Lally, Paul Budd, Nick McCoy, Sandeep Kumar, Richard Armeson, Jake Timothy, Scott Baker, Sarah Overend, George Anderson, Richard Tuson, Mike Branagan-Harris, Anne Rhodes, Lucy McCarraher, and Daniel Priestley and the Dent/KPI team of entrepreneurs and mentors. Daniel is an incredible entrepreneur and I would recommend his courses to anyone interested.

Special thanks goes to Diane Irvine, someone I met initially as a young, inexperienced sales person on one of her courses and who has helped and inspired me in many ways since then, particularly in the last two years.

Thanks also to everyone who helped to review the manuscript of this book at different times and at different levels of completeness, who wrote testimonials, who offered ideas and insights and who contributed towards its completion. Richard Thomas, Colin Smith, Susan Holland, Diane Irvine, Stephen Kemp, Becky Blackwell, Ceire Rochford, Isaiah Hankel, Jonathan Penny, Matt Seago, Jon Daswon, Niall Barry and Andrew Rowlatt. Particular thanks to James Lumsden-Cook and the team at Bennion Kearny for their responsiveness and professionalism in bringing these ideas to life.

Thanks to all my old colleagues at Vygon, DePuy and Align Technology, many of whom I stay in touch with and who continue to make me feel part of an extended team, and Raphael Pascaud who remains the most talented business leader I've had the pleasure of working for and who provides me with direction and insight without even realising.

To my current team who help me to think with greater possibilities and create increased opportunities – Mark Davies, Lynsey Ross and Nikki Webber. In addition, Brigitte Bell whom I first met 16 years ago, who married one of my best friends and now is a huge part of what we do – including all of the illustrations in this book. Also, thanks to Jag Shoker, the best coach in the world.

Finally, thanks to my wonderful wife and business partner – my soul mate on this rollercoaster of a journey called life. Andrea is my biggest critic and biggest supporter and the ideas in here are as much hers as they are mine. She gives me everything for which I'll always be grateful, including my three beautiful children Henry, Charles and Alexandra. I love you all.

Thank you to everyone who gives me the opportunity to do what I do. I am incredibly grateful.

ABOUT THE AUTHOR

Michael graduated from the University of Leeds after completing a BSc in Medical Biochemistry. After taking up a sales role in a medical device company, he quickly established a successful career in the industry, which saw him appointed to numerous sales and marketing management roles across three multi-national companies, most recently as Director of Sales for Europe.

In 2010, Michael was awarded an MBA with distinction from the University of Warwick where his final dissertation focused on strategies for market entry. In 2012, Michael completed his Professional Certificate in Coaching at Henley Business School.

In 2012 Michael co-founded Developed Edge, a training and development organisation that works specifically with medical companies to help them identify the best way to sell to their customers and then create customised and competency based training programmes.

In 2014 Michael published his first book, GO NAKED Revealing The Secrets Of Successful Selling which went on to become a number one best-seller. Since then he has also published over 100 articles, e-books and reports. He also works as a Coach, Speaker and Advisor.

You can connect with him directly via:

Email: michael@gonakedselling.com

Twitter: @smith_michaelj

Facebook: www.facebook.com/gonakedselling

You can also read his weekly blog at www.gonakedselling.com

TABLE OF CONTENTS

Dedicated to all those people who get up in the morning to work hard to serve their customers and their organisation, who pride themselves on the value they create, who think in terms of possibilities, and who strive to create opportunities and to pursue a better way.

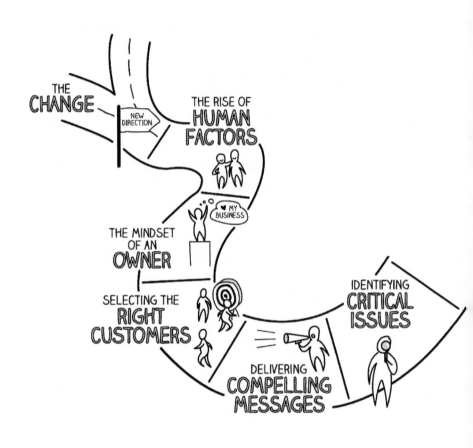

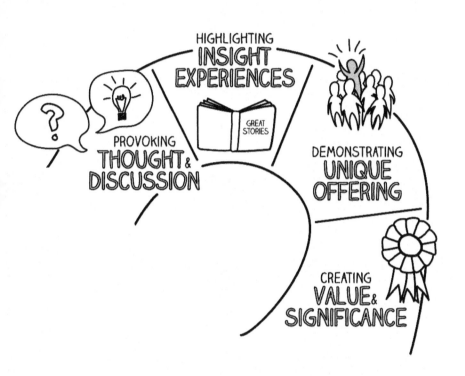

PROLOGUE

The journey around London's South Circular Road is a challenging one at the best of times. But in early morning rush hour traffic, the journey from Beckenham to St. Thomas' Hospital – that is less than ten miles and should only take around 45 minutes – can take closer to two hours.

In order to reduce the time associated with commuting in London, I would tend to leave home at 6am and arrive into St. Thomas' for around 6.45am. This gave me ample opportunity to sit down with a coffee and some breakfast and complete the administrative tasks associated with being a sales professional working for a medical device company in 2003.

Everything was in triplicate – one copy for me, one for my boss, and a copy for the office. Although laptops and mobile phones were now commonplace, we were a little behind the times. Paperwork that was a requirement of the role was exactly that – paperwork. Expense claims, daily call reports, weekly and monthly journey plans, call analysis, sample requests – everything was written by hand on carbonated paper and posted at the end of the day.

At that time, the minimum expectation was that we completed 12 calls per day. 12 face-to-face appointments with customers within a single account. That meant a minimum of eight hours in the hospital but often and due to the traffic, this became a ten and 12-hour day.

The products we carried were a range of single use anaesthetic, critical care, and general medical products. From theatre disposables to cannulae and intravenous extensions lines, we had a broad portfolio. That was the company's strategy. Go wide.

I'd been fortunate to find a job straight from university but, quite honestly, had fallen into sales. I'd originally wanted to join the police force and for one reason and another, that hadn't materialised, and so I was left, in my final year at university, not knowing what I would do with my time when the social and academic vacuum of life away from the University of Leeds became a reality.

Receiving an email from the University's career's forum, I'd seen one with a subject that read, 'inexperience essential'.

That was definitely for me.

Other than part-time student jobs and a three-year degree course in medical biochemistry, I had no vocational experience to speak of.

The promotional email was for a recruitment agency that specialised in graduate sales jobs. The relatively lower cost of the graduate's employment combined with their drive and determination to escape student debt made them an attractive proposition for companies looking to expand their sales team and their business.

Covering the length and breadth of the UK, from manufacturing to IT, to finance and the medical industry, they served a broad spectrum of clients. I passed their assessment, met their selection criteria and, due to my degree type, was sent for an interview with a medical company.

That was some 12 months ago and now, sitting here in St. Thomas' Hospital, I reflected on the apparently ordered randomness of life that had led to me sitting, drinking coffee in a hospital foyer, about to embark on my 12 calls for the day selling single-use medical products.

The Reality Of Rejection

By 11am, I was four calls into my required 12 for the day.

It had been a disaster.

Everywhere I went, I was rejected.

The pre-ordered, pre-determined sales script was falling on deaf ears. No one was saying the right thing. No one was giving me the answers they told me I would receive. Dragging my wheelie-case down another flight of stairs, I headed directly for the car park.

I'd had enough.

When I'd arrived at 6.45am that morning, mine was one of only a handful of cars occupying the spaces. The staff had their own car park, and very few other non-staff had any reason to be at a hospital at 6.45am. Now at 11am, the scene was different.

In the middle of the morning, with scheduled appointments, out-patients clinics and visiting hours in full swing, my black Vauxhall Vectra was hidden against the array of others cars now surrounding it.

Still, that's where I was headed.

I opened the boot and threw my bag into the back. It bounced momentarily before coming to rest against a sample box and expandable folder full of product literature. I pulled the heavy boot down and made my way to the driver's side door. Opening it, I collapsed into the seat, pushed it back and closed my eyes.

What was I doing?

Getting up at 5.30am to be in a hospital for 6.45am, to sit and do paperwork before having my sales script rejected in every call. Whilst my friends had gone travelling or taken jobs at large professional firms, I was doing this. Badly.

There must be a better way.

Right there and then I made a decision.

I would find a better way.

I would commit myself to the perpetual learning, development, understanding and application not just of sales approaches but business approaches.

I wanted to be seen as the *credible expert*. Someone customers would value as an industry peer. A professional they would look to for knowledge and advice, for help and support and to connect with others within my network. I wanted to understand business, practice the key elements of sales and marketing, and show that a sales person wasn't just someone out there pushing unwanted product and reciting a sales script, but someone making a tangible difference to the people they worked with.

I wanted to demonstrate – initially to myself and then to others who doubted it – that the role of the sales person wasn't just a noble profession but a critical one; one that, without its very existence, would leave business lifeless.

Every enterprise needs sales.

Every business needs sales people.

And what if there was some way of seeking greater possibilities, increased opportunities and a better way?

INTRODUCTION

In 2014, I published *GO NAKED: Revealing The Secrets Of Successful Selling*. As I considered the model and the contents of that book, there were three key elements that I knew when writing that book that still hold true today.

Firstly, that for any approach to anything to be successful, there needed to be a certain philosophy or mindset. Secondly, that regardless of the product or service, it is the people involved that make the difference. And thirdly, there needed to be an impactful process.

The content of that first book was very much about the former two – a philosophy based on my experience of what the top 10% of sales performers in the industry do differently to ensure success. Not what they did 10 or 20 years ago, but what they're doing now. In the new world we live in.

One of the questions that came up after some people had read that book was, 'it sounds great, I really enjoyed it, but how do we ensure that we apply it on a daily basis?' As a result, I worked with a range of individuals and teams on how to turn the ideas contained within the book into reality.

As I planned out what this next book would be about (the one you now hold), I considered this question: 'How do we ensure that we apply it on a daily basis?' And as a result, I've tried to make this second book much more practical and immediately applicable. This is what you might call 'the process part'.

This book is designed to be a thought-provoking and practically applicable book.

I hope it stimulates discussion, cultivates new ways of doing things, and makes a tangible difference to the people and businesses that individually and collectively read and apply it.

But let me get back to the part about a process versus a philosophy.

Whilst the first book was about a philosophy for sales, this one is far more about the steps or the process required.

Now I appreciate that the word 'process' sounds robotic and mechanical. I don't mean it to. It's merely that it's the best adjective I have to articulate that there's a need for a considered approach to anything – particularly sales.

For whilst it's easy to get focused just on the result (after all, that's what we're all measured on), focusing only on the result, the numbers, or the sale isn't going to change anything.

It's the same as a Formula One team working to improve the speed of their pit stops. Yes, the time taken is what they will be assessed against, but a focus just on the time won't change anything. It's the activity, the steps, the constituent parts of the process that can be developed to ensure a better outcome.

Likewise, the sports coach standing by the field of play knows the score and will be assessed against the result. But focussing on the score doesn't change anything.

It's what happens on the field of play which matters.

It's what happens on your field of play that matters.

The activity is something you can control. And it's the activity that determines the result.

The truth is that there can't be 100 best ways of doing something. It just doesn't work that way. And sales is the same. There's a core set of ideas that, if applied effectively, can make a difference in the world in which we now operate.

As with everything, though, I don't expect anyone to adopt the ideas in this book with 100% replication, but to adapt them in a way that works for them.

This book is not designed to be an independent approach or one that fundamentally goes against the principles contained within the first book. In fact, it's very much in keeping with those themes – I see the *GO NAKED* principles as the fuel that powers this process. So rather than focussing first on the transaction or the sale, then finding ways to help and support before finally being seen as a valued advisor, we need to flip that model and instead focus on ways to create value first so that the transaction or the sale follows as a consequence.

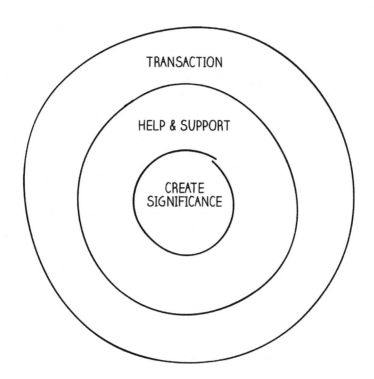

For the first time in history, it's not the product, the features and benefits, or the solutions that will make the difference, but the individuals – the sales people – who provide the greatest single point of differentiation.

15 or 20 years ago, companies would baulk at this assertion, and it would be met with the rebuttal, 'Our sales people can't be our differentiating factor. Because what happens if they are and they leave?'

Now my answer is simple, 'What happens if they're not and they stay?'

That's even more of a problem.

There are a lot of unknowns out there for all of us. Globalisation, nationalism, the political landscape, the economy; the market and industry in which we work is turbulent.

However, what I do know is this: the world isn't changing. It has changed.

Fundamentally.

Old-school sales techniques are outdated, and anyone employing them will soon be outdated too.

Need satisfaction selling.

Solution selling.

Feature-benefit selling.

Pump and dump, pre-determined sales scripts.

They're history.

What is required for success in our new economy are people who acknowledge their role as project managers, as professional change creators; those highly skilled people who can identify the right individuals to work with, who deliver Experience Insights, adapt their messages to their audiences, and who create value and significance.

Does that sound like you?

If those few words and ideas 'click' with you, if they resonate with you, and if they sound like they could describe the way you work – or hope to work – then what we'll do over the remainder of this book is explore a structured approach to a set of key steps that will allow you to amplify each of them, to become even better at them, and become a top performer in your role.

Then, as with everything, it's over to you.

The book is split out into three parts.

Part 1 – How You Think, Act, And Interact

Part 1 looks at the mindset required of the modern day sales professional, and the term I use for that person is *'Intrapreneur'*. It considers the changes required as a result of the changing market and the role the sales professional now plays in creating value and significance. And it considers the role of the system in which we operate, and how it influences our outcomes through a set of factors associated with human behaviour.

Part 2 – Driving The Customer Conversation

Part 2 lays out a six-step process to take a potential customer on a journey, through identification and winning time, to framing the conversation, provoking thought and discussion, and demonstrating your experience before highlighting your Unique Solution.

Part 3 – Becoming The Credible Expert

Part 3 breaks down the idea of creating value as part of the purchase experience to a set of key roles and activities that the sales person must adopt in order to succeed in the new economy and become The Credible Expert.

I hope you enjoy this book.

I trust it will provoke some thought and that on reading it, you'll do something differently – even just one thing – which impacts you, your customers, and your business.

I wish you continued success, as you become The Credible Expert.

PART 1 – HOW YOU ACT, INTERACT, AND THINK

The world into which we sell has changed and acknowledging that change is a crucial first step. We must strive to harness the power of personal responsibility; combined with an open and creative approach to possibilities we will create greater opportunities. By skilfully navigating the complex human system we operate in, we can further develop our relationships and commercial outcomes.

HOW YOU ACT – THE CHANGE

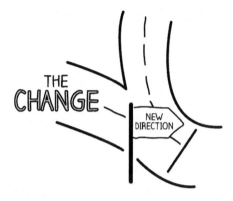

People provide the greatest opportunity for differentiation in the market

CHOICES AND TOLERANCE

Imagine sitting, reading this book. Not today, but in the early 1900s instead.

Okay, you'd be a little freaked out having ordered it online or when reading it on your tablet or smartphone, but putting that aside for a moment and suspending your disbelief, a couple of things would be true.

Firstly, if you'd graduated in 1920, you'd be one of only 4,357 students[1] to have obtained a first degree in the UK that year – this during a period when the economy shifted from one being fuelled by agriculture to one driven by manufacturing.

It was the era of the rise of Ford and the inception of mass production – of assembly lines and factories. In addition, you and I, in the early 1900s, would be hoping that our kids would leave school and get a steady job, working in one of these new and magical places. Factories had become the engine of that time, and you either worked in one or owned one. Either way, they dominated the economy.

In an era when material possessions were based on and chosen by necessity rather than desire, choices of product and services available to consumers were limited and tolerance of sub-optimal performance or customer experience, on the other hand, was high. After all, when you have a choice of one, what's the alternative? When you can have it in any colour you want, so long as it's black, then that's the one you'll take.

So in business, we began to think about our assembly line – the customer assembly line. It turned out that once customer-facing people had acquired so many customers or accounts, they could no longer sell and service to the same extent. And so the roles were now differentiated, and the first breakthrough occurred.

Our sales organisations become factories as roles were broken down into their constituent parts, and those tasks were assigned to different people. As a result, growth began to accelerate.

Fast-forward some 30 or so years to the next generation and by 1950, some 17,337 students [2] obtained a first university degree in the UK. There was an upward trend in the number of 'qualified' people in the country. Not only were the traditional factories creating more products, but the factories of education were also creating more (people) products.

In post-war Britain, business and babies were booming, and there was a shift from manufacturing to management and professional roles. In other words, with more people in work, there was the need for more managers to manage.

Consequently, from working on the factory line, the next obvious step was to become the one in control of the line. The person managing the line.

And so, at that time, we'd be encouraging our children to leave school and get a job with the aim of becoming a 'manager'. It was the advent of the white-collar worker, but university was still reserved for a relatively privileged few.

As this shift occurred, it's no surprise that business journals such as the Harvard Business Review (HBR) started to gain popularity, as did writers such as Peter Drucker, the famous management consultant. With more managers out there, the idea of management – and leadership – became more popular as did the desire to learn more about it. As growth in industry accelerated, so did the idea of what it meant to manage, to lead and serve consumers.

This, coupled with a rise in innovation, led to a series of changing dynamics.

More jobs meant more money in the economy, which led to more choices for the consumer.

No longer were we constrained by a choice of one.

More money, more products, more desires, more consumption.

Two income families meant 'Keeping up with the Joneses'.

More products, more features, and more benefits. Find out what the customer needs and then match it with any of the broad array of features and benefits we have. Everyone needs something. Everyone needs more! And so feature-benefit selling was born.

By 1956, the first computer hard drive was used – in a protected environment – and was able to store a little under 4MB of data.

(As an aside, this hard drive took up a space about the same size as a hotel room!) And in 1960, Theodore Levitt wrote his much acclaimed 'Marketing Myopia' paper. In this seminal work, he described the need for diversification – businesses should offer more choices to their customers and potential customers.

Change was on the horizon.

As was more choice.

Shift forward again to the next generation and in 1980, some 68,150 UK students [3] obtained a first university degree, and the tide was beginning to turn as advances in technology and education started to break down once seemingly impermeable barriers in connection and growth.

The professions – medicine, law, accounting and business – had gained popularity, as had the financial industry. No surprise then that the movies 'Wall Street' and 'The Wolf of Wall Street' were both set in 1987 as commerce changed, hot off the back of the first Personal Computer (invented and commercialised in 1981 by IBM) which transformed the efficiency of the financial system.

Life was about to change altogether.

Consider what we'd want at that time for the next generation and the likelihood is that we'd want our kids to move into professional or commercial roles where the chance of higher salaries, benefits, and options would be more prevalent. As more companies expanded, we were greeted with ever more choice and the finances to support them.

And life became all about solutions. What solutions could we offer to people? As technology advanced, so did the belief that we could bundle our products or services in a way that would create a compelling customer solution that would be significantly better than the single entity product or services being sold by our competitors.

And now move to the present day, or close to it. In 2011, 350,800[4] students obtained a first university degree in the UK – an exponential rise in graduates when compared to the previous generation. In 2014, the iPhone 6 was released amidst some of the greatest and fastest-changing technological advances ever. In the palm of your hand, you could hold more technological power than a whole room could have contained a few short years earlier. More qualified people out there were vying for more professional jobs, more management jobs, and more leadership positions. All able to connect – instantly.

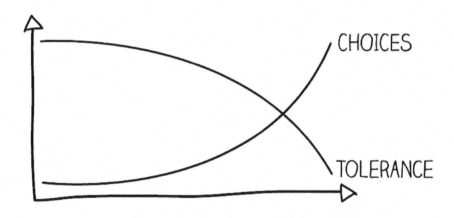

Barriers to trade, connection, and commerce were practically extinguished and for a few hundred pounds, anyone could be equipped with the means to start a business or make a connection thanks to social and digital media.

In a relatively few short years, we've gone from the Ford Model T to the first hard drive, to the personal computer, to social media and smartphones. Who would have thought that, in 2016, we'd hold enough computing power in our pockets to start movements, businesses and social trends? And obtain the answer – almost instantly – to almost any question.

Was it the technology that changed society or society that drove technology?

As a result of technology, power has shifted away from manufacturers and suppliers. In an economy of choice, the consumer is met with a greater number of choices than ever before, while accompanied by a lower than ever tolerance. Lower tolerance for the average, the mediocre, and the sub-optimal.

And so in sales, the tide has shifted again. No longer is it about organisational structure, features and benefits, or solution selling, but – as witnessed over the last few years – it has become more and more about personal connection, the purchase experience, and the role of the salesperson as a valued advisor.

If the 1920s was about agriculture to manufacturing and the changes in organisational structure...

If the 1950s was manufacturing to management and the rise of feature-benefit selling...

If the 1980s was from management to professional and commercial and the bundling of solutions...

And if the first decade and a half of the 2000's has been about a rise in connection and the role of the salesperson as a valued advisor...

Where does that leave us moving forward?

INFORMATION AND TIME

Think about the same timeline, the same shift through the generations.

Whilst choices and tolerance have moved in opposing directions, so too has information – the accessibility and quantity of information – and the amount of free time to assimilate that information.

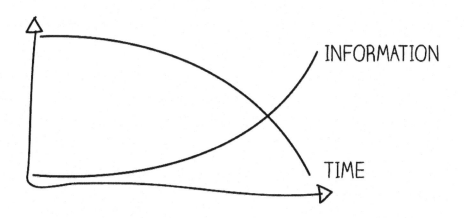

When information was far less ubiquitous, knowledge was only as good as the information that was presented. To a large extent, we were governed in our knowledge by the people we interacted with – which was why academic and learning institutions were so critical. Meet someone, take the information, become informed. If you were a well-informed, knowledgeable person with the resources to match, then you held the metaphorical aces.

In business, customers would wait until their salesperson arrived to provide them with the latest information on the newest product or service. They were reliant on the company and its representatives coming equipped to sell features and benefits that would meet a 'need'.

'The need'.

Perhaps the most overused expression in business and sales, and the thing we've all been searching for. The Holy Grail. The customer need.

But now, in our modern world, the process no longer works like that.

You don't have to attend an institution or wait for the right person to call by to get information. You ask Google. And what's more, it's free.

Now we gain knowledge through multiple sources often simultaneously. We are as informed as we wish to be and, in the event that we require or desire more information, it is only a click, tap, or swipe away.

The only reason someone isn't well informed today is because they choose not to be.

Remember this as it's an important fact underpinning this shift, and the way we now need to approach our customers.

Today, we're no longer constrained in our knowledge base by the people we know but by the time we have available in order to consume more and more information from a plethora of sources. But it's that time – our free time – which has proportionally reduced. We have access to more information than ever before. We have less time to assimilate that information than ever before.

The customer needs someone who can help to cut through the noise and address this challenge. The customer needs The Credible Expert.

WHERE TO FOCUS FIRST?

The thesis of *GO NAKED Revealing The Secrets Of Successful Selling* was that by focusing first on ways to create significance, by acting primarily to create value for the customer, the transaction or the sale would then follow as a consequence.

The alternative model – the traditional selling model – developed in the 20s, 50s, and 80s (prior to our ultra-connected, hyper-informed world) was a model based on the fundamental principle of selling and then supporting. It identified a customer need and then showed how your product or service could meet that need and, importantly, how it did so faster, cheaper, or better than the competition.

It was us versus them.

The relative features and benefits of one product, versus the relative features and benefits of the next.

And that worked fine in the old economy when choices were limited, and tolerance was high.

When it was a question of your product versus the next, and it was a straight-out fight for A versus B, then salespeople held more information than their customers, and they were the ones in control.

However, that model assumed four important pre-requisites:

1. The supplier knew more, and was better informed, than the customer

2. The decision-making unit was simple and one-dimensional, with customers making decisions based on independent needs

3. The customer had a choice to make between only a small number of options

4. The customer could accurately articulate their product or service 'needs' which could then be supported or matched by relevant features and benefits

Contrast that to our current reality:

1. Customers are as well, if not better, informed than the majority of suppliers

2. The decision-making unit is now a complex matrix of interconnected stakeholders with multiple requirements

3. The customer now has endless choices between many options

4. Customers' worlds are complex interactive systems where what they are looking for (short-term gain) and what they need (long-term sustainable change) are not necessarily the same thing. They often aren't driven by product and therefore the feature-benefit conversation doesn't provide a compelling reason for change

This new reality means that – as sales professionals – we need to adapt our approach to sell in an aligned way to market challenges and organisational priorities within our more informed and complex customer base.

Choices are now high whilst tolerance is low.

Information available is now high whilst time available is low.

Something had to change.

Something has changed.

A FOUNDATION FOR CHANGE

The best salespeople I know – many of the best salespeople out there – already acknowledge and understand the impact of these changes and are focused on creating value or significance first; they have already adapted their approach.

However, the foundation – that traditional model of feature-benefit, need satisfaction selling, and solution based selling – whilst a platform from which to build, is nothing more than that. A foundation.

It offers only table stakes – the minimum required to take a seat at the table and compete – and does not lead to a point of differentiation against the myriad of choices available.

A recent study by the Corporate Executive Board [5] suggested that 53% of a customer's buying decision was based on what was described as the Purchase Experience. The Purchase Experience included a range of activities which sales professionals could undertake including:

1. Providing unique insights, particularly with regards to the economics associated with the product or services

2. Teaching customers about new issues impacting the market

3. Helping customers navigate alternatives

4. Helping customers to avoid mistakes, risks, and pitfalls

5. Providing customers with the opportunity to interact with, network through, and gain support from peers

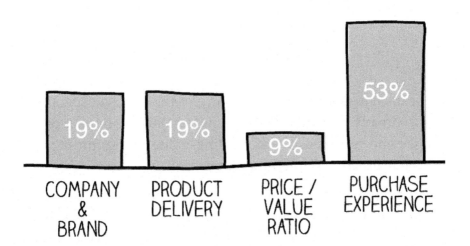

These elements – many of which are representative of the core components of the salesperson adopting the role of a Teacher, Coach, and Facilitator (TCF) – are not evident or taught in traditional needs-based sales training and require the sales professional not only to work to promote their company's product or service, but also to serve their customer base in a way far more evident in a service business than a product business.

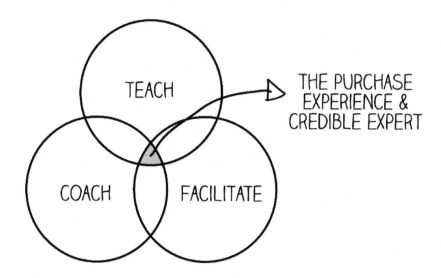

It's perhaps no surprise that in the 1970s and 1980s, during the rise of the needs-based selling approach, manufacturing was responsible for double the proportion of economic output than it is today. At a time when our world was led by products rather than services we operated in an age when customers had a narrower range of choices and had the capacity for greater tolerance. This dynamic was set against the reliance upon the supplier to be the keeper and provider of information and customers weren't constrained by the sheer strain on their time from the constant flow of information. At this time, then asking the question 'What's the most important thing to you?' and then presenting a series of relevant features and benefits seems (on reflection) to have been an obvious approach.

But the world has changed.

The alternative lies in identifying themes or issues of possible interest to the customer; those associated with goals, objectives, problems, or challenges. It requires us to research those themes or issues linked to relevant market and industry information and explore their current and future impact on the customer (before offering up Experience Insights, relating this to their world, and then linking them to possible opportunities for change). I describe these themes as Critical Issues.

In reality, the subtle change is from asking 'what's important to you?' to provoking thought and discussion around what we know to be important. Through the identification of Critical Issues and then exploring and creating opportunities around them, we have the chance to frame the discussion from the customer's perspective.

The requirement now is that the sales professional is no longer someone who asks for change but someone who provokes change. And so practically, it means flipping the traditional question of 'what's important?' to knowing, identifying, and highlighting 'what's important'. The thesis is a simple one: getting the customer to *think* differently will more likely get them to *act* differently.

This is not to say that a deep understanding of the product or service isn't essential – it is. It's just that in-depth product knowledge is table-stakes. In other words, they provide us with the minimum required to compete in the marketplace – **and only that.**

What is likely to set you apart – as a company, team, or individual – requires resourcefulness, thinking in terms of possibilities, creating opportunities, and taking ownership of the business.

Given the increasing complexity of the market we sell into, in the coming chapters, we'll explore the steps that the modern sales professional needs to master.

We'll consider the extent to which the onus has shifted from the customer to the supplier as the one who needs to take on the responsibility for the sales journey; an approach to ensuring that we're identifying the right customers to spend our time with.

We'll consider how we get in front of customers and would-be customers, how we deliver issues, themes, and messages that provoke thought and discussion, how we explore their Current and Future States, and how we demonstrate our credibility and offering. Finally, we'll consider practically how we create value and significance, and differentiate ourselves from the competition.

For the first time in history, it isn't the organisation, product, or services, features, or benefits that offer the greater point of differentiation, but the people. The salespeople. People like you and me.

KEY MESSAGES

- The world that we sell into has fundamentally changed because of two sets of opposing forces:
    - Choices and tolerance
    - Information and time
- Customers have more choices than ever before but less tolerance for the average, mediocre, and sub-optimal
- Customers have access to more information than ever before but are overloaded. They have less time to assimilate the information available
- Salespeople need to adopt the roles of teacher, coach, and facilitator as a way to create value and significance

- Focus first on these areas so that the sale or transaction will follow as a consequence

- For the first time in history, the biggest point of differentiation isn't the product, the service, the features and benefits, or the organisational structure. It is the salesperson

HOW YOU INTERACT – THE RISE OF HUMAN FACTORS

Involving others is crucial to achieving success

HOW IT BEGAN

On Sunday, March 27th, 1977, two Boeing 747s collided on the runway of Tenerife Airport in what is still the worst accident in aviation history. Through the horrific loss of life that was suffered that fatal day – a total of 583 people were killed – what followed was a complete overhaul of the processes and frameworks used in aviation.

The result was a considered appreciation of the complex interactions that exist in aviation between the environment, people, communication, leadership, and decision-making.

The interaction of those key parts in the system we call life are known as Human Factors.

Since then, the discipline of Human Factors has played a core role in aviation training and, more recently, has become more prominent when hospitals consider their approach to patient safety. Martin Bromiley, a commercial airline pilot, has led the charge to raise awareness of the considerable benefits of an acute understanding of the role of human factors in healthcare. [6]

What is apparent, however, is that these factors – these same human factors – exist and play a crucial role whenever there is an interaction between people and their environment. Understanding the perceptions of others, and the nuances of human nature, also form part of the differentiating factor in what allows great sales professionals to stand out in their industry.

During our discussion, we'll refer to four Human Factors pillars that underpin successful selling:

1. Situational awareness

2. Communication

3. Personal leadership

4. Decision-making

THE FOUR PILLARS

SITUATIONAL AWARENESS

Situational awareness refers to the ability to assess the world around us accurately. This could be with respect to the environment, with regards to other people, or the specific situation and our evaluation of it. It requires us to gather information from these various sources, to identify what information is important, to adjust our thought process, and then to respond accordingly.

Having a keen situational awareness is something that is apparent in people who have a high degree of emotional intelligence as they gather information, notice, and identify the changes required and then respond.

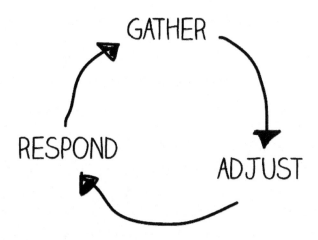

Imagine the salesperson who is excluded from selling into a particular account due to a competitive contract being in place. Consider the one who ignores the conditions and goes about their business regardless. The person who walks into operating rooms and clinical areas and who shows a lack of appreciation of the previous work done in that account and by the key stakeholders – the same key stakeholders they hope one day will buy their product or service. The person who is focused on short-term gain, who manipulates customers and tries to conquer within the term of the existing contract, despite clear guidance to the contrary.

Compare this to the salesperson who has acute situational awareness. The salesperson who spends time gathering information and positioning their activity in order to present the most commercially compelling offer to the account when the contract period is renewed. The salesperson who adjusts their thinking to take a long-term view and is proactive in creating future opportunities. They respond with understanding and empathy to the essential work done by their customers.

The difference between the two is based on strong situational awareness.

COMMUNICATION

Communication within Human Factors rests on three components – that the communication is clear, complete, and mutually understood. For communication to be successful, all three elements need to be in place. In fact, consider it to be a tripod where, if any one element is missing, the structure would be unstable and collapse. So, in terms of our self-assessment, we need to consider the extent to which our communication is clear, complete, and mutually understood.

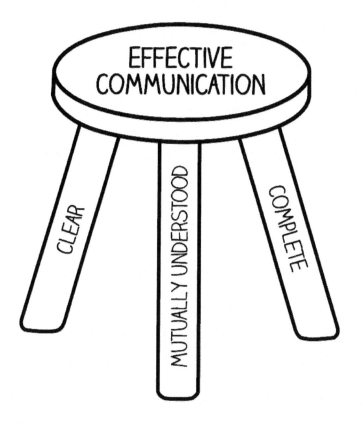

Picture the salesperson who leaves their meeting 'knowing' what will happen next. That the customer has (in the salesperson's mind) committed to the order or the evaluation. The customer, on the other hand, believes that they have done no such thing, but merely agreed to consider the idea; they believe that the next step is a further discussion with other key stakeholders. The salesperson leaves the meeting and informs their sales manager that the business will be in by the end of the quarter.

The potential for breakdown at multiple levels (salesperson to customer, salesperson to sales manager, sales manager internally, and so on) is now worryingly likely due to the Gap in expectations which now exists as a result of communication not being clear, complete, and mutually understood.

Compare this to the salesperson who leaves the meeting only after checking that each person is clear on the next step, has a complete and mutual understanding, and who confirms each step in writing shortly after the meeting has ended to ensure that their discussions and next steps are mutually agreed.

The difference between the two is based on the factor of communication.

PERSONAL LEADERSHIP

Personal leadership applies in many areas but, at its heart, requires each person to be willing to step forwards, to be brave, and to take ownership of a situation. It requires each person to abandon inertia, indifference, and apathy. It means seeing something that might possibly be changed, identifying an opportunity for improvement, and then doing something about it; a choice is made whether to be reactive or proactive, passive, or assertive.

When you're standing in a clinical area and you see a clinician about to use your product incorrectly, or off-label, what do you do? Do you stand up and say something, clearly articulating in a calm and confident manner the issue you've noticed? Or do you keep quiet, hope for the best and keep your fingers crossed that it'll all be okay? Or does it depend? Will you sometimes just see how it plays out?

Acknowledging this type of scenario as a chance to create an opportunity demonstrates a high level of personal leadership. Conversely, denying or ignoring this as an opportunity demonstrates a low level of personal responsibility.

All of this is a key pillar within Human Factors – that of personal leadership.

DECISION-MAKING

Improved decision-making comes from being better informed. Being better-informed results from doing two things. Firstly, involving others in the decision-making process, and secondly, following a process of divergent to convergent thinking. In others words, whenever a decision needs to be made, following an initial period of thinking creatively, in terms of the possibilities, before prioritising and finally assessing the most viable way forward.

When you consider a goal or objective, what's your first step? Do you get straight into the planning, or the doing?

If you're like most people, defaulting straight to activities and tasks is our natural position. Particularly in sales. We find that salespeople are very outcome and task focussed, and so our more comfortable position is based on getting on with the task in hand. However, the alternative is to think in terms of possibilities *before* prioritising and planning.

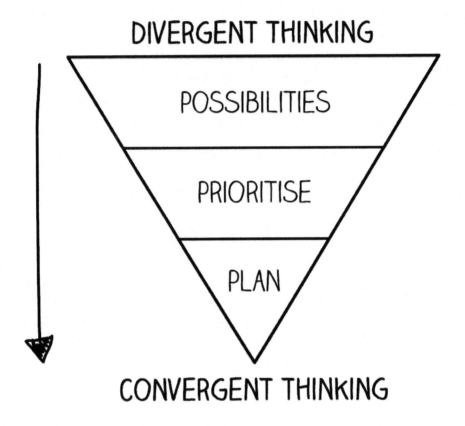

DIVERGENT THINKING

POSSIBILITIES

PRIORITISE

PLAN

CONVERGENT THINKING

When there's a decision to be made, how do you approach it? Do you involve others or go it alone? Do you put your 'arm around your work' for risk of others getting a glimpse of your ideas, your thinking, your brilliance, your frailties?

Do you pause and consider alternatives? Do you actively seek out new, improved, better ways of doing things?

Or do you stick to the path most travelled and apply the same decision-making to new problems.

Your willingness to do any of these things relies on the Human Factor that is Decision-making.

So let's pause for a moment and consider each of these in turn.

Think about the examples above. How would you rate yourself on a scale of 1-5 (1 being low, 5 being high) in terms of your ability to effectively demonstrate great:

- Situational awareness: ___
- Communication: ___
- Personal leadership: ___
- Decision-making: ___

Now plot each of your scores on the grid below.

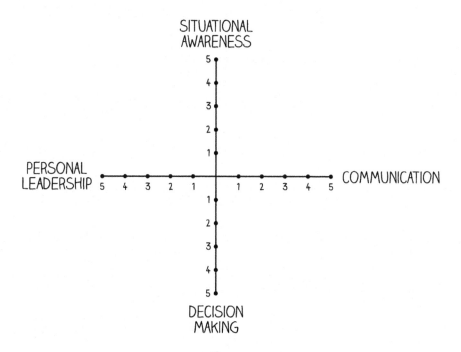

As you look at this, where do you currently excel? Where do you need to do some work? How do you compare to the maximum score for each of the four pillars?

What does this tell you about you and your development?

APPLICATION IN OUR MODERN COMMERCIAL WORLD

As we work through the rest of this book, it's not my intention to turn you into an expert on the theory of Human Factors, but I do hope you become expert at noticing – in any given scenario – the extent to which you are effectively managing those human factors; the things that affect each stage of the selling journey.

This stuff is important. It all links to emotional intelligence that has been shown time and time again to be a point of differentiation in business.

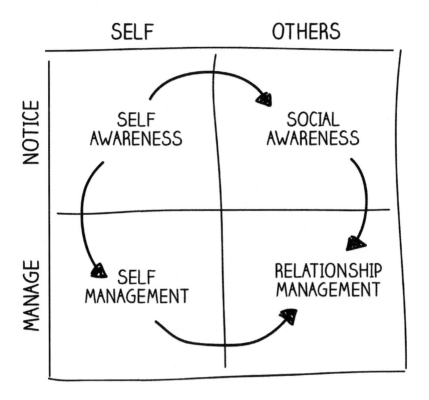

Intelligence or technical ability only get you so far. The thing that is more important than intellect, when it comes to the development of successful customer relationships and successful selling, is emotional intelligence – in other words, the ability to identify, use, understand, and manage emotions in positive ways to relieve stress, communicate effectively, empathise with others, overcome challenges, and defuse conflict.

So when you consider the illustration above, the outcome of emotional intelligence and its different parts is improved relationships. This begins, however, with self-awareness, which is why being able to notice signs and signals in yourself first is so important.

Research carried out by the Carnegie Institute of Technology [7] showed that 85 percent of your financial success is due to skills in what they called 'human engineering': your personality and ability to communicate, negotiate, and lead. Only 15 percent is due to technical knowledge. Additionally, Nobel Prize winning Israeli-American psychologist, Daniel Kahneman [8], found that people would rather do business with a person they like and trust than someone they don't, even if the likeable person is offering a lower quality product or service at a higher price.

So take the time to notice the extent to which you are considering the role of human factors – of Situational awareness, Communication, Personal leadership, and Decision-making in your daily decisions and the outcomes that they produce. And importantly, be willing to involve others in your thinking, prioritising, and planning.

KEY MESSAGES

- Human Factors is the study of people and their interaction with the system in which they operate

- There are four key pillars which form the collective of Human Factors

  o Situational awareness

  o Communication

  o Personal leadership

  o Decision-making

- Being able to notice when each of these elements plays a role, particularly during significant interactions, provides the opportunity to progress towards a more positive outcome

- There are strong links with emotional intelligence and the importance of self-awareness and self-management – of noting and managing yourself and others

- As we do not operate in a vacuum, we should actively involve others in our thinking, prioritizing, and planning

HOW YOU THINK – THE MINDSET OF AN OWNER

Those who consider greater possibilities create increased opportunities

AN OWNER'S MINDSET

There has been much talk by business commentators and writers about the growth of small businesses and entrepreneurialism. At times, it's perhaps easy to think (given some of these ideas) that we should quit our jobs and run headlong into a new venture expecting it to be fundamentally different to our previous roles.

Whilst the chance to start a business undoubtedly provides opportunity and fulfilment for some, it is not the be-all and end-all, certainly not for everyone. It is most definitely not a better or worse option – merely an option.

There is perhaps a perception that one is easy whilst the other is hard. That one is safe, whilst another is risky. Or that one is right, and the other is wrong.

However, my belief – having done both – is that neither is any easier or harder, safer or riskier, or better or worse. They're just different. And each is based on fit and personal preference.

Isn't there always a 'but'?

Yes.

The 'but' is that there is no difference in the above, so long as your ultimate goal is to be the owner of whatever your particular kingdom looks like. Whether that be a job, a role, a project or initiative, a territory, region, country, or something bigger. In addition, our 'jobs' as sales professionals shouldn't revolve around a task-orientated tick-list, but be a matrix of interconnected commercial projects. And that's the case, regardless of the product or service we sell.

Those people who perform well and who are successful, regardless of their title or operating structure, have a number of key attributes in common. A range of key success factors that allow them to excel and achieve. These people are 'intrapreneurs'.

THE RISE OF THE INTRAPRENEUR

So that we're clear on this, let me start with a definition of an Intrapreneur:

An Intrapreneur is a person who works effectively with others, who takes direct responsibility for the success of a project or initiative; of turning an idea into a profitable outcome through assertion and innovation.

Let's consider some of these key elements in turn and how they might possibly apply in your daily role.

Works effectively with others

This person works within an organisation. Big or small, it doesn't matter. Over-resourced or under-resourced – that's not important. This person is part of a team and works with the team. They actively seek to involve others and leverage the available knowledge base.

Takes direct responsibility

Regardless of their title or role, this person proactively takes direct responsibility for the outcome. They don't wait to be told and they don't rely on other people. They're the ones who will put their neck on the line to make sure it happens. They are creating their own map rather than following someone else's.

Is success and outcome-orientated

The outcome of anything will be measured by its success. Therefore this person can define what a successful outcome will look like and be able to answer the question, 'how do you know you have been successful?' The type or size of the project or initiative doesn't matter and isn't defined by job role or function.

Ensures a profitable outcome

One of the aims of the business is to maximise profit, and this person understands the critical role they play in that journey. That means that in the pursuit of any commercial outcome, they are cognisant of the profitability of the initiative, not only with respect to the direct revenue and cost associated with the final outcome but also the cost associated with its pursuit and the relative opportunity costs. After all, they could be somewhere else, doing something else. But they're not. They've made a choice to pursue this particular outcome.

Assertion

This person is confident and driven. They are results-orientated and make things happen. Where others may stumble, the Intrapreneur is focused on the outcome and adjusts their activity in order to ensure that it is optimal. Importantly, though, they know when to quit and move on. Understanding that their time bears a cost, they select their opportunities wisely.

Innovation

Perhaps the defining feature! Innovation requires creative thinking, exploring new ideas, considering possibilities first, and ensuring divergent and open thinking. In addition to looking 'outside the box', the focus is on 'the edges of the box', the place that author and entrepreneur Seth Godin defines as being innovative and creative, and where the outcome is also within their sphere of control.

To assess your current level of Intrapreneurship, complete the table below.

For each of the above areas, score yourself on a scale of 1-5, 1 being low and 5 being high.

What is your intrapreneurial score?

Factor	Score (1-5)
Works effectively with others	
Takes direct responsibility	
Is success and outcome orientated	
Ensures a profitable outcome	
Assertion	
Innovation	
Total (Add the scores above – max. 30)	
Percentage (Divide score by 30 and multiply by 100)	

- *What does your score tell you about you and your development?*

- *Which area do you already excel in?*

- *Which area do you need to develop?*

- *What is your next step to develop this?*

Whatever your score, it's clear that in the new economy, it's these traits and behaviours which are likely to aid the successful salesperson.

If the sale is no longer one-dimensional and, to a large extent, requires the salesperson to manage greater complexity and increasing numbers of stakeholders, then the ability to demonstrate and develop each of these areas will be key.

Whilst people may talk about ownership and responsibility, it is bringing each of these areas to life that makes the difference.

SEEKING AND CREATING OPPORTUNITIES

The extent to which we're willing to take on personal responsibility and demonstrate the traits of the intrapreneur is proportional to the outcomes or the results – the ability to make a difference.

Take a look at the illustration below, which plots personal responsibility against the ability to make a difference – and the correlation to our view of 'opportunity'.

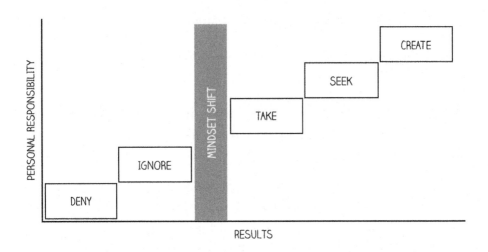

Adapted from Andy Gilbert, 'Go MAD – The Art of Making a Difference' [9]

Andy Gilbert [9] is the most effective I've come across at describing the interaction between personal responsibility, opportunity, and results.

At the lowest level of personal responsibility, the chances of someone making a difference are low, if not non-existent. As a result of this, they are likely to *deny* that an opportunity exists.

You've seen the type of person. You tell them about an opportunity with a particular customer or account, and they tell you flat out, 'no'.

'No, they're not interested. They've never been interested. They never will be interested'.

Nothing happens, as no intrapreneurial traits are demonstrated.

At the next level up, there's a marginal increase in personal responsibility, but again the likelihood of making a difference is limited. This low level of personal responsibility is associated with a view of *ignoring* opportunities.

That person may say they'll follow up that interested customer. They may go and visit that lead, but when you ask them what's happened a month later, nothing's changed. They've just ignored the opportunity.

At this point, and certainly for most people who stay in and are successful within a sales role, a mindset shift occurs and, at a minimum, they are willing to take opportunities as they are presented. Although it could still be considered as reactive, when an opportunity arises they *take* it; they do it and deliver.

However it's at the next two levels, the top two levels, where the greatest degree of personal responsibility is demonstrated, the biggest difference is made, and individuals *seek out* and *create* opportunities.

They demonstrate those characteristics we previously associated with intrapreneurialism – *working effectively with others, taking direct responsibility for the success of a project or initiative; turning an idea into a profitable outcome through assertion and innovation* - and the results speak for themselves. And this is now the playing field of the modern, successful sales professional.

So when I talk about personal responsibility, ownership, intrapreneurialism and developing these areas, what I'm also saying is that it's those people who proactively seek out greater possibilities who will create increased opportunities and with them, their chances of a successful outcome.

As you consider what it means to be an intrapreneur, to demonstrate a high level of personal responsibility, there are three important elements to consider:

1. An abundant mindset
2. Knowing it's possible
3. Personal reflection

1. An Abundant Mindset

Imagine two accomplices locked in separate jail cells; each offered three choices by the police. One: if both confess to the charges, both will be jailed for five years. Two: if only one confesses, he will be freed, but the other (the non-confessor) will be jailed for ten years. Three: if neither confesses, both will be tried for minor offences and jailed for only one year each.

If both accomplices know that the other will not treat the police offers as a competition, that there doesn't need to be a winner and a loser, then instead, they can take their collective interest into consideration, and they can both win.

But how often does this happen?

In game and economic theory, a zero-sum game is a mathematical representation of the conditions under which this occurs – that a participant's gain (or loss) is exactly balanced by the losses (or gains) of the other. To put it differently, total gains plus total losses would have to equal zero. Or another way, for me to gain the sale, you have to lose the sale.

If I assess every situation, opportunity, project, sale, or initiative as a zero-sum game, then I'm making the assumption that in order for me to win, then you have to lose. Conversely, I'm assuming that in order for you to win, I have to lose.

Contrary to this theory, the idea of non-zero-sum describes a scenario where the participants' aggregate gains and losses equal more than zero. And in this situation, one person's loss (or gain) doesn't equal another's gain (or loss).

In other words, we can both win.

This is an abundant mindset.

The problem we have is that, for the most part, we assume that our world, and particularly our business world, operates under zero-sum conditions. And to some extent, that's the way we've been taught and conditioned to think that business and selling works.

Right, I'm going to do that before you do. Otherwise I may lose!

If on the other hand, we strive to work under the conditions of a non-zero sum game, then the actions that we take will vary dramatically. If I'm not assuming that for you to win, I lose – and vice versa – then I'm likely to operate in a very different manner. My thinking will be different and, as a result, the things I do will be very different.

And it's these actions that sit at the heart of the idea of abundance and a 'win-win' mentality, versus the idea of scarcity. The notion that there isn't enough opportunity out there for you, me, and everyone else is only true if I'm operating under zero-sum conditions.

The challenge with abundance and a non-zero-sum game is that there is no universally accepted solution. There is no single optimal strategy that is preferable to all, and no predictable outcome. In some instances, we'll have mutually aligned objectives and in others, they'll be contrasting.

But the salesperson who assumes a higher level of personal responsibility, who strives for abundance and win-win scenarios, is able to live out the behaviours associated with the concept of a non-zero-sum game in pursuit of mutual and shared success.

2. Knowing It's Possible

Of course, it may seem impossible, and often it feels like it is, especially in our new and complex selling environment:

- *Converting that competitive account...*

- *Changing the practice of that one, difficult, prospective customer...*

- *Turning around the fortunes of a failing business or territory...*

- *Setting up a new business or territory in a competitive environment, or*

- *Managing a difficult relationship*

In the moment, all of these challenges – and many more – can seem impossible and can lead you to think that, actually, it's probably better to give up and look elsewhere for something easier.

However, there are some important questions to ask:

- *Has anyone ever converted a competitive account before?*

- *Has someone ever changed the practice of a difficult customer before?*

- *Has anyone ever turned around a failing business or territory before?*

- *Has someone ever established a new business or territory in a competitive environment before?*

- *Has anyone ever successfully managed a difficult relationship?*

The answer, of course, to all of these is, 'yes'.

But the fact that the answer is 'yes' is actually more important than a first glance may suggest.

In knowing that something difficult has been done before, in knowing that a challenge or obstacle has been overcome, and in knowing that people – and many of them – have prevailed in difficult circumstances, you know that it is possible.

As you look at your business, give some thought to the number one challenge you could solve, and take solace and assurance from the fact that someone, somewhere, has successfully navigated a similar challenge before.

Because once you know it's possible, it completely changes your mindset and perspective and leads you onto the next important question:

If I know it's possible, how can I make it a reality?

3. Personal Reflection

As sales professionals, one of our most essential skills is the ability to self-analyse.

If we don't consider how effective we are, then we run the risk of doing the same thing over and over again. No change. No development.

If everything we did were successful, then repetition would be fantastic.

Yet it seldom is – for the simple reason that our environment constantly changes.

We can borrow ideas, but we can't borrow situations. So it's only through the application of ideas that we have the opportunity to learn.

Our ability to evaluate how well we achieved a task, or whether we achieved it at all, is a key factor for success.

Self-analysis separates the mediocre sales professional from the great one. Self-reflection is key.

A major indicator of a high level of emotional intelligence is your ability to reflect on your performance, and to analyse how well you did.

- *What gets measured gets done*
- *Inspect what you expect*

So if we measure something then we're saying to others and ourselves: *'this is important'*.

Sales managers are an excellent resource – they can provide you with insightful comments about how well you performed in front of the customer. And a good sales manager will act like a mirror, allowing you to reflect on what, and how, you performed in each of your sales interactions. A good sales manager is a coach, through whom we become better salespeople.

Unfortunately, though, our sales manager can't travel with us all the time. So how can we continue to hold up that mirror when travelling alone? There are three simple steps to becoming an ever-evolving sales professional, one who adapts to the changing environment, capable of overcoming new challenges as they arise.

And it involves asking some reflective questions:

What did I do well in that call?

It is important that we ask this question of ourselves first.

Humans have a tendency to focus on the negative.

We punish ourselves for the things we did wrong.

In his book *The Inner Game Of Tennis* [10], Timothy Gallwey talks of how, after making a mistake, we mentally ask ourselves:

- 'Why did I do that?'
- 'I always do that'
- 'I'm no good at that'

And it becomes a self-fulfilling prophecy.

The 'self-talk' we give ourselves determines the mental attitude we carry with us.

So focusing on the 'helpful and constructive' maintains the mental attitude and worldview required of successful sales professionals.

By asking 'what did I do well?', we frame our mindset as positive. And we should follow up 'from the things I did well, what will I carry forward and do again in future calls?'

The phrasing of the next reflective question is important.

And it is not 'what did I do badly?'

If I were to do that again, what could I possibly do differently?

Notice the subtleties of the change in language. Asking oneself about doing something differently and doing something badly have very different effects on our psyches, our mindset, and our next steps.

Acknowledging what 'could possibly be done' allows the mind to open up and explore options; to build on what went well and identify where opportunities lie.

It is creative and experiential and allows you to picture the future.

The final stage in the self-reflection process is to ask:

What do I commit to do again which will help me in the future?

Now the next part is important. Really important.

Write down, in ink, the answers to your questions.

In writing the answers down, you will make a tangible commitment to yourself.

Some people I've worked with even send these to themselves as an email, SMS, or postcard with a delayed delivery date or mail them to a trusted colleague.

Holding yourself accountable to achieving this, significantly increases the chances of you doing it.

The difference between winning and losing is not much.

In all competitions – sporting events or in business – it is those who take time to ask themselves the question 'how can I do this even better next time?' who are the ones who develop a personal 'winning culture'.

In order to analyse, we must record our successes as well as the things we need to improve. We must consciously repeat the activities that bring us success and identify when activities do not work – and have the confidence to experiment with ideas and approaches until they do work.

YOUR OWN HIGH-PERFORMANCE CULTURE

A culture is a result of the constituent parts – the people – that combine to form an organisation. Companies spend millions on trying to develop, create, change, and reinforce cultures, but the fundamental truth is that you can't change an organisation's culture, you can only work to develop the individual cultures. It is the sum of the parts that is greater than the whole.

People talk about 'a high-performance culture', but that is a direct result of the degree to which individuals accept personal responsibility and own their business. Leaders can take steps to increase ownership through autonomy, mastery, progression, and purpose, but ultimately it's down to the individual. It's down to you.

In our modern selling environment, we all need to be project managers, managing multiple projects at any one time. Regardless of the size of company or team, that requirement is a constant. We need to set goals, establish teams, involve others, set timelines, establish accountability, and measure outcomes. But those things require the mindset of an owner.

This idea of ownership is critical because, without it, all the tools and techniques in the world aren't going to have the same impact as they otherwise could.

The rise of the intrapreneur means that there is a window of opportunity for the sales person who can seek out and create opportunities; who thinks abundantly, thinks in terms of possibilities, and who is willing to do the (often difficult) emotional work of personal reflection. At a time when the single biggest point of differentiation is the salesperson, the intrapreneur has the opportunity to be that difference.

KEY MESSAGES

- Inextricably linked to success in the modern selling environment is having the mindset of an owner – the mindset of an intrapreneur

- *An Intrapreneur is a person who works effectively with others, who takes direct responsibility for the success of a project or initiative; for turning an idea into a profitable outcome through assertion and innovation*

- When we consider the link between personal responsibility and results, we must acknowledge that there are five levels which exist – deny, ignore, take, seek, and create

- There are three essential factors that contribute to the mindset of an owner:

  1. An abundant mindset

  2. Knowing it's possible

  3. Personal reflection

- Embracing these factors and this mindset leads to the development of a high-performance culture

PART 2 – DRIVING THE CUSTOMER CONVERSATION

In our complex selling environment, we must first identify the right customer before delivering a compelling message that differentiates us from the competition. By framing the conversation from the customer's perspective, we provide an opportunity to engage in a thought-provoking and change-enabling discussion. Customers like certainty and to picture the future, and we can assist them in this through our experiences. To affect change, our product or service must link back to their Critical Issue.

SELECTING THE RIGHT CUSTOMERS

Our focus determines our results

A SHIFT FROM THE ONE-DIMENSIONAL APPROACH

When I first learned to sell, the recommended approach was a relatively simple one.

We would identify the person who was responsible for using the product, ask them a series of funnelled questions to identify their 'need', provide the relevant features and benefits of our product in order to satisfy or support their need, and then ask them for the order.

Some of the time that worked fine and other times it worked badly. When the decision-maker was the user, and when the user placed the order, perhaps that was a reasonable approach. Often, in the late 90s and early 00s, the person we called on was the butcher, the baker, and the candlestick-maker. We had one person to identify, and once we had, our job was half complete.

Contrast that to now, though, with the complex selling environment we face and the significant changes that impact business-to-business sales. As we considered in Part 1, as salespeople we are much more akin to 'project managers' who are being asked to manage multiple commercial projects in parallel. And one of the skills of the effective and successful salesperson is identifying those people involved in an often broad and varied decision-making unit.

As our focus determines our results, it is essential that we identify those people who are most likely to positively impact our commercial objective and then take steps to get their individual and collective buy-in to the sales journey for which we're responsible.

Even within that, there's an ever-expanding matrix of people we could see, which, coupled with our (often) unwillingness to step out of our comfort zone, means that it's incredibly easy and understandable either to spend time with the wrong people, or fail to identify the range of possible stakeholders who can support the achievement of our commercial objective. Ironically, we become busier than we've ever been before.

What we're going to explore over the remainder of this chapter is the importance and application of *Selecting The Right Customers*.

QUANTITY, QUALITY, DIRECTION

If you look at any sales process, one of the easiest variables to measure is activity associated with productivity or quantity. For example, the number of visits, calls, demonstrations, and presentations are all things that are measures of quantity of activity.

In other words, 'are you doing enough stuff?'

Of course, the other option is to look at quality measures, which are based on outcome. It might be the amount of knowledge retained by a customer at the end of a demonstration, the performance of the company at the end of an evaluation, the feedback from a customer at an educational event, or the willingness of a customer to commit to the next step.

All of those things are quality measures.

In other words, 'are you doing the right stuff, in the right way?'

Sometimes we can fall into the trap of thinking that it's an either/or situation and that it's either right to focus on quantity (are you doing enough stuff?), or to focus on quality (are you doing the right stuff in the right way?).

What we can see from the chart below is that the net output from too great a focus in either of those areas can actually be the same, and that the far more profitable place is to get a balance between quantity and quality of activity.

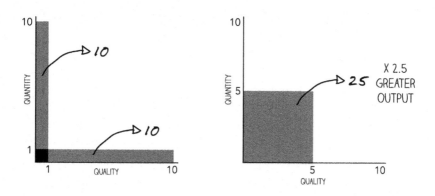

When we do enough activity in the right way, the net output is far greater than an unequal focus on either variable.

The third variable to consider is the direction, or the focus, of the activity. This could include the account you visit, the department you focus on, or the customer you identify. The direction or focus is usually a 'place' or a 'person'.

In other words, 'doing enough stuff, the right stuff in the right way, with the right people.'

Which brings us back to our original objective and statement: *Selecting The Right Customers.*

STAKEHOLDER MAPPING

Models are great because they provide a structure to frame our thinking. And that's important because it's our thinking that drives our activity and ultimately our results.

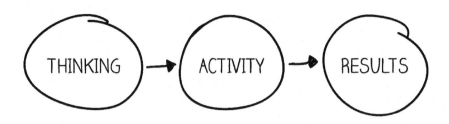

Stakeholder Mapping is an approach which should be utilised whenever there is a key goal or objective to be achieved within a complex selling system. It is particularly useful in key accounts, large accounts, when new to an account, or when there are multiple groups or individuals involved, such as for a combined business contract or tender.

The process of Stakeholder Mapping is the method by which you develop a profiling matrix, identify your key stakeholders, and develop plans to win their support. It allows you to consider all the possible stakeholders before determining your priority stakeholders. Who you include in this group will depend on your particular goal or objective, and it provides the opportunity to set the direction of your activity based on a more robust assessment of the possible commercial stakeholders.

SIX STEPS OF STAKEHOLDER MAPPING

The process of Stakeholder Mapping follows six steps that run sequentially and should be completed in order:

1. Define Objective
2. Consider Possible Stakeholders
3. Map Power, Interest, and Influence
4. Map Relationships
5. Identify Groups
6. Select Right Customers

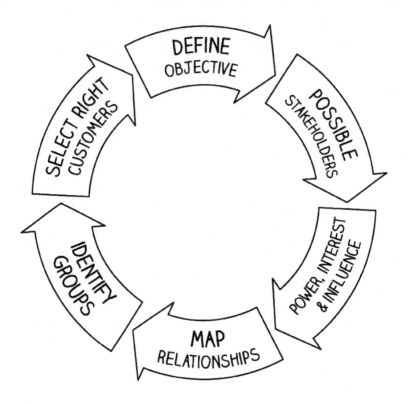

Before we get into the detail of each step, it's worth considering the following questions:

- *Have you ever had an objective or account that has stalled?*

- *Have you ever had an objective or account where it's been incredibly difficult to make progress towards your goal?*

- *Have you often struggled to determine who the right person to see might be?*

- *Have you experienced the challenge of seeing the same person repeatedly but not made real progress towards your goal or objective?*

If the answer to any of these questions is yes, then it's likely that the process of Stakeholder Mapping could help.

In order to get the most of out of this section, I would suggest taking a read-through first and then revisiting each step and digesting further. The process we'll work through will provide you with both an opportunity and a template to apply this model to an account or objective.

1. Define Objective

I've previously talked about the importance of understanding your 'why' when it comes to setting goals. Knowing why you're doing what you're doing, and being clear about it, is what's likely to keep you going when times become tough. Whilst SMART goal setting isn't necessarily a tool to increase motivation, it is the best tool to provide clarity on what you're going to do.

With that in mind, let's define what SMART means:

- Specific: What specifically do you want to achieve?

- Measurable: How will you know you have achieved it?

- Achievable: How strong is your belief that it can be achieved in the time available?

- Relevant: How does this goal contribute to higher Account/Territory goals?

- Time-bound: What is the deadline for completion?

Being able to answer each of these questions is a crucial step in the achievement of anything. However, in the process of Stakeholder Mapping, it is a defining step, because you will link back to it at various other stages in the process. Getting clarity on this will also determine those people you might see, and the extent to which they carry relative power, interest, and influence.

2. Consider Possible Stakeholders

In a business-to-business context, (purchase) decisions are often made collectively. Suppliers find it important to know who the most influential person in this process is. The whole team of decision makers is known as the Decision Making Centre (DMC).

At this point in time, it's not about defining exactly who to see, but considering who you might *possibly* see that could support your objective. This requires you to do some investigation and research, to ask questions, and to seek out and involve others – both internally and externally.

In fact, a great question to ask at the end of every meeting with a stakeholder is, *'Who else might possibly be interested in a project like this?'*

The language we use here is crucial. The words 'might' and 'possibly' lend themselves to people thinking creatively and openly without feeling wedded or committed to the answer. In addition, the use of the word 'project' creates a sense of team, of ownership, and of something that's more than just a one-dimensional transactional sale.

Make it your goal to leave each meeting with an answer to that question.

Remember that the groups, departments, or individuals you need to access will vary depending on your particular objective, so make sure that you are considering possible stakeholders in the context of your objective, not simply your product or service.

For example, the people you would need to see for an account-wide conversion would most likely be different to the people you would need to see for a single department conversion.

The following seven categories are all worth considering as you ask yourself, *'Who else might possibly be interested in a project like this?'*

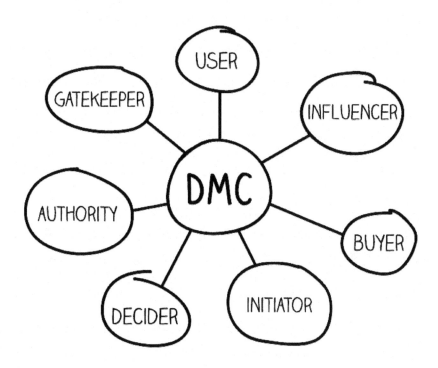

- The User – the person(s) who will be the primary user of the product or service

- The Influencer – the person(s) who may not use the product or service but whose opinion may impact the perception of the User

- The Buyer – the person(s) responsible for the ordering or processing of the product or service

- The Initiator – the person(s) who recognised the need for change and initiated the process

- The Decider – the person(s) responsible for the decision

- The Authority – the person(s) responsible for the budget

- The Gatekeeper – the person(s) who forms a barrier to entry into the process, and who controls access to any of the above individuals

There may be instances when an individual can occupy more than one role and not every category of person will be present in every buying scenario. However, it helps to frame thinking by considering the relevance of each role and the individuals who may be present.

Once you have considered each of these groups, departments, and individuals, the next step is to assess and map their power, interest, and influence.

3. Assess And Map Power, Interest And Influence

The variables with which we choose to assess the attractiveness of any particular group of customers could be based on any number of variables that allow us to objectify what is ordinarily a subjective decision. We will base our assessment on three criteria:

1. Interest
2. Power
3. Influence

In our definition, *Interest* is the extent to which they care about your defined objective. In other words, are they bothered?

Power is based on formal criteria and is often associated with seniority, and can be the result of authority, hierarchy, or title.

Influence is less formal and is the result of the person's connections and strength of relationships. They may not have direct power – the ability to sign the requisition – but they may certainly be able to influence the outcome.

Power and Interest should be scored on a scale of 1-10, 1 being low, 10 being high, whilst Influence should be scored on a scale of 1-3, 1 being low, 3 being high.

The data on each stakeholder should then be inputted into a table similar to that below to provide an initial assessment of individual power, interest, and influence, and also the relative differences between the individuals. More often than not, once this initial assessment begins, it provides opportunity for discussion and consideration as to who actually has the power, interest, and influence.

STAKEHOLDER	POWER	INTEREST	INFLUENCE
David Jones	7	4	3
John Smith	3	9	1

4. Map Relationships

One you have your stakeholders rated for each of the three variables, that data can be transferred to our Stakeholder Map and placed in the appropriate place on each of the two axes – power and interest, with the size of the bubble denominating their level of influence.

None of these individual stakeholders exist as an island, but in an interconnected system. Therefore the next stage is to map out those inter-connections and the direction of influence. This allows you to assess not only who to prioritise in terms of their power, interest, and influence, but also their ability to affect the wider stakeholder base.

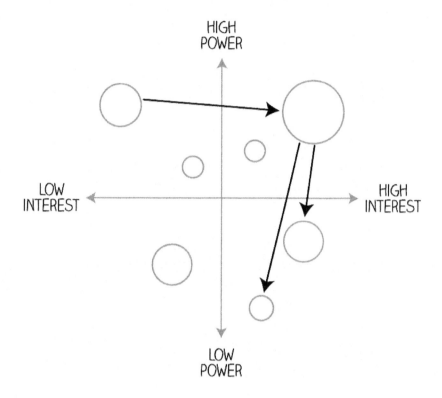

Again we see why the question we asked earlier is so important: 'Who else might possibly be interested in a project like this?"

And when you have an answer, ask a follow-up question such as, 'How might you possibly work together with them on this type of project?' Again, we're using the language of possibilities, creativity, openness, and team.

5. Identify Groups

Once you have your stakeholders mapped against the variables of power, interest, and influence, and their relationships connected, you're now in a position to consider how they might group together.

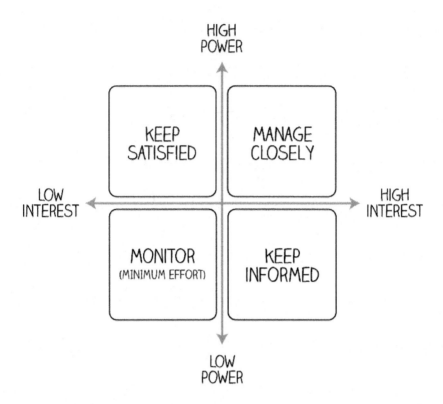

The purpose of grouping our customers is to answer the question, 'out of everybody available that we *could* spend our time with, who *will* we spend our time with?

The insights we glean from their position on these interest and power axes can give us a far more objective assessment of how we undertake our selling activity within that account.

In order to label our quadrants, we're going to use a sporting club analogy. So we have our Managers, Coaches, Players, and Owners.

1. High interest and high power – The Managers

2. High interest and low power – The Coaches

3. Low interest and low power – The Players

4. Low interest and high power – The Owners

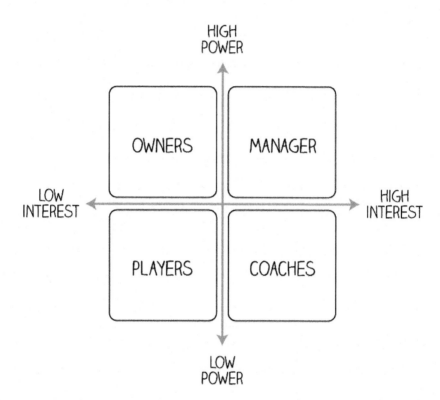

In the upper right-hand corner, we have our *Managers*, those people who have high power and high interest in our commercial objective and are likely to make something happen. They have commercial control and, assuming our objectives are aligned with theirs, they are interested in supporting our cause. Note that although we classify them here as 'managers', that doesn't mean that they will necessarily be a 'manager' in role or title.

Consider the sporting analogy. It is the sporting managers who are ultimately responsible for day-to-day operations and who have the control to make the majority of decisions.

In the bottom right-hand corner, we have people who hold high interest but low power. They are our *Coaches*. They've bought into our objective but they have no formal power to make the decisions. That's not to say that they can't be an ally – they can – it's just that they aren't going to drive the process.

From a sporting perspective, the Coach is a critical part of the overall team, but their focus is more on supporting any process or decision-making rather than guiding it.

In the bottom left-hand corner, we have people who are low interest and low power. These are the *Players*. They'll turn up no matter what and do what is asked of them. They prefer to steer clear of the commercial objectives and whilst they may hold influence internally, they aren't significantly involved in the decision-making process.

Consider a sporting team. The players play regardless of the politics. The get paid and perform and don't traditionally steer decision-making. Whilst there may be some exceptions with senior players or team captains, these people occupy only a quasi-management role.

Finally, in the top left, we have people who are high power and low interest. These people are the *Owners*. And it's our goal to find them and spark their interest. These are people who we really need to watch carefully, because although they may not initially be interested in our commercial objective, they have the power to make a difference to its outcome. We need to manage this group of people very closely.

In the context of a sporting club, the owners ordinarily hand over operational control to their managers. They can veto any decision due to their power, and will usually be guided by the thinking and consensus of their managers.

Once these people have been put into their groups, that is the end of our grouping process. Now we need to consider, out of those possible groups of people that we could spend our time with, where will we focus our activity.

Note here that the assessment of the individual's power is, at this stage, more important than accurately assessing their level of interest. This is due to the fact that power is not a variable that we have any real opportunity to influence. Interest, however, is something that we can influence, and in those instances where we should engage with the Owners, then part of the task is to increase their level of interest.

6. Select The Right Customers

Will we spend our time with the people in the top right, the bottom right, the bottom left, or the top left-hand corner of our matrix?

In reality, it's going to depend not just on the group that they fall into, but their connections to other people and the extent to which we believe they can influence the outcome. What we do through this process is move away from using terms such as 'important'. We become able to identify both customers and potential customers, and to consider the relative merits of spending time with them versus others.

In this instance, we use our three variables of power, interest, and influence, to take something that is subjective and make it more objective.

For those people in the top right-hand corner (Managers), we should manage them closely. In the bottom right-hand corner (Coaches) we should keep them informed. In the bottom left-hand corner (Players) we should monitor them, but with minimum effort, and in the top left-hand corner (Owners) we should keep them satisfied. Of course, the size of the bubble represents the size of their influence with one being small and three being high.

So we know there are clear links between sales activity and performance, and that activity should be broken down into three components: quantity, quality, and direction. Stakeholder Mapping allows us to group customers into potential groups, giving us the opportunity to decide who we will spend our time with. The process that we need to follow is to define our objective, to think in terms of possibilities, and then to map our priorities and create a value plan.

Start With The End In Mind

How we frame our thinking, and the activity which follows, should all be based on our commercial objective. How that varies will determine the likely people involved and their willingness to engage and participate.

However, this isn't a fixed process but a dynamic one; one which changes over time, and evolves as our understanding of the environment and the people involved changes.

By developing a framework for our thinking, we start to turn what is often a subjective approach to the question 'which *customers should we spend our time with?'* to a more objective approach, which considers the variables most likely to determine our selling journey.

Once we've selected the right customers, the next challenge is to begin to engage with them with a view to gaining time for a discussion or meeting. And this is one of the most common questions we hear today. How do we win time with a key customer?

The Touch System

To win time with key customers, we need to find a way to stand out from the competition. Rather than asking for an appointment or meeting, the key is to give something instead; something of value so that you begin to become significant in your (potential) customer's mind.

In 2011, Google commissioned a piece of research into how customers make buying decisions and coined the term, 'Zero Moment of Truth'. [18] The Zero Moment of Truth refers to the period between a stimulus and the customer making a decision to buy. Based on the research, they found that, on average, customers needed 10.4 interactions before making a purchase decision.

From a sales perspective, we refer to these interactions as 'touches' – and so we're aiming to develop a system that allows 11 interactions over a three-to-six month period. This is known as a Touch System.

A Touch System is a way to break down the value you will give to a key customer into a series of planned interactions. The plan needs to include two elements – the activity, and the communication route.

These activities that create value could be varied but should be significant. Articles or summaries of articles of interest, industry publications, legislation, guidance, benchmarking, testimonials, or educational invites, to name but a few. Communication routes could be post, face-to-face, email, phone, message, Facebook, LinkedIn, Twitter, and so on.

A hospital business manager recently said, 'I don't usually give time to industry representatives, but I am willing to. The reason I would give a sales person time would be if I thought they could help me to achieve my goals or objectives. So I'd be looking for them to begin engaging with me – perhaps sending me information that is relevant to my market, organisation, or role, or identifying things that they thought I'd be interested in. I wouldn't meet someone because of the product they sold but because of the help they could bring.'

This is an incredibly powerful approach, and it requires us to:

1. Select activity that creates value and which positions the sales professional as the Credible Expert

2. Develop a series of 11 touches

3. Plan to deliver regular and consistent value over a three-to-six month period

4. Vary the communication route

In doing so, you position yourself away from the rest of the competition as someone who gives value first before asking for a meeting, appointment, or sale. You begin to position yourself as the Credible Expert.

KEY MESSAGES

- As a result of the change in the selling environment, the decision-making unit that we have to engage with is broader and deeper

- This requires us to objectify the subjective in terms of how we identify who we choose to spend our time with

- Our sales activity can be broken down into three areas – the quantity (or output), quality (or outcome), and direction (or focus)

- It is our thinking which drives our activity which drives our results, and so we must think differently before we can expect a change in our activity

- Stakeholder mapping provides a way to segment customers into distinct groups and to consider who best to target our time with

- Stakeholder mapping considers three variables – power (formal), interest (in our commercial objective), and influence (informal)

- There are six steps to undertake in order to successfully stakeholder map:

    1. Define Objective
    2. Consider Possible Stakeholders
    3. Map Power, Influence, and Interest
    4. Map Relationships
    5. Identify Groups
    6. Select Right Customers

- Once we have selected the right customer, we can then consider how we create value and significance

- We use a Touch System to win time with key customers and to demonstrate value

DELIVERING COMPELLING MESSAGES

The clarity, uniqueness, and purpose of our message ensures that customers become advocates

PICTURE THE SCENE

Imagine that you are in the elevator and you're on your way to visit a customer. As the doors open, a key opinion leader enters the lift and says 'Good morning' to you. 'You look like you're in sales, what do you do?'

You've been trying to get an appointment with this person for months.

I want you to picture being in that scenario and imagine what you would say, and how you would articulate a compelling message, in order to secure additional time or a meeting.

This is a really important question to ask and an even more important question to answer: to give some consideration to how you would really articulate what your message and what your value is, and to stand out from the crowd by delivering a clear, consistent, and compelling message.

It's clear that we've all got a huge amount of value both as individuals and as organisations, but to think that the product speaks for itself, or the features and benefits speak for themselves, is really far too short-sighted, particularly in our changed selling environment. If we accept that there is very little to separate the functional performance of most of the top products, then it follows that it is the salesperson who provides the single biggest point of differentiation. And so we need to communicate that message with clarity.

Over the course of this chapter, we are going to consider the importance of winning time and being memorable, so that in the example of the scenario above, you have a clear structure and a methodology to be able to do both. We'll consider some of the common errors that we make when answering the question 'What do you do?', and we'll look at the different components that are included in a proven approach in order to answer that question.

Being memorable is important in any context, but certainly in business-to-business sales. In a particularly crowded market where there is a huge amount of choice in terms of product and suppliers, when the information available is so comprehensive, and when there are so many salespeople vying for the customer's attention, then standing out is even more important.

It sounds like a cliché, the idea that first impressions count and that being memorable is important, but it's a cliché for a reason, and that's because it's true.

We used to think that people make judgments within the first three to seven seconds of meeting somebody and that a variety of assumptions are made about that person. However, new research suggests that those judgments are made almost instantaneously. [11] Those assumptions can be based on any number of factors including appearance, facial expression, body language, mannerisms, demeanor, tone of voice, and the language which is used; but customers are no different and the impact that a person can make in such a short space of time shouldn't be underestimated.

The Mehrabian Communication Model [13] demonstrates that 7% of the impact of communication is down to the actual words that are spoken, 38% is due to tone of voice, and 55% is down to body language.

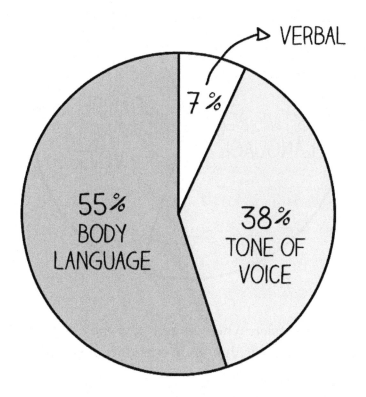

Now that's not to say that any one of those one elements is something that can be avoided. I'm not saying that the spoken word is insignificant; it is absolutely crucial. All of the parts of the system are required in order to constitute the whole. The clearer the verbal message, the more compelling the tone of voice, and the more positive the body language, the more your customers will experience greater congruency between the spoken word, tone of voice and body language, resulting in far greater impact overall.

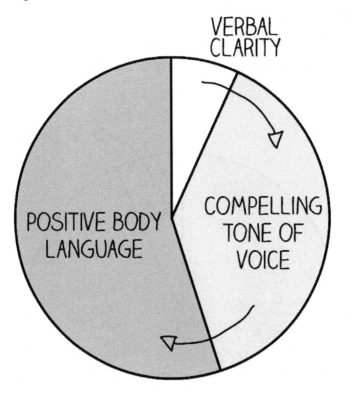

Often it's much easier, when we're asked the question 'What do you do?' or 'What is it that your company does?', for us to fall into a trap where we just list out a number of features and benefits and where we focus first on the product.

Perhaps we might even just get into discussing irrelevant information or use corporate buzzwords; words that mean something to us but which mean very little to the person who we are talking to. We talk in a way which fails to consider the audience and their requirements. When we meet with a stakeholder, a potential customer, or a customer, it's important that we do a number of things:

- Make an impact
- Take control of the conversation
- Give them a reason to speak to us again
- Engage with them enough to win time with them again

If we consider many of the greatest wealth creators and change makers in history, many of them started out with a powerful statement which opened and engaged discussion with individuals and groups, and with little more than their words and their statements they were able to start movements, trends, and affect social norms.

Some examples of these historical statements are:

'I have a dream that one day this nation will rise up and live out the true meaning of its creed: We hold these truths to be self-evident: that all men are created equal' Martin Luther King Junior

'We chose to go to the moon in this decade and do the other things, not because they are easy, but because they are hard' John F. Kennedy

'We'll put a computer on every desk and in every home' Bill Gates

'Every moment wasted looking back stops us from moving forwards' Hillary Clinton

'You must be the change you wish to see in the world' Gandhi

'Imagine all the people living life in peace' John Lennon

'Where there is discord, may we bring harmony. Where there is error, may we bring truth. Where there is doubt, may we bring faith. And where there is despair, may we bring hope' Margaret Thatcher

'If man goes to the moon we'll go there too, open a restaurant and serve him a great burger at a great price' Ray Kroc

'Share a daily dose of inspiration with women all over the world' Oprah Winfrey

So how many of those did you know? How many of those stand out in your mind? How many of those had you heard or read before?

Whilst we may not be in the business of presidential races, personal computing, spiritual leadership, or fast food restaurants, these examples show that simple words can be turned into powerful statements that bring clarity to the listener and to the audience, not only about what that person stands for, but why we should continue to listen to them.

WHAT, HOW, AND WHY

There are three things which are important to consider – three definitions which we need to be clear about.

The first is **core capability**. The core capability is the activity that the business performs at a consistently high level and which is essential to its success and competitive position. In other words, this is 'what' you do.

The second is the **unique differentiator**, the factor that differentiates a product or service from its competitors, such as being the most efficient, the highest quality, or the finest ever product of its kind. This is 'how' you're different.

And finally, the individual or company's **purpose** – this is the reason for its existence, its intention, or its objective; its overarching aim. This is 'why' someone should work with you – either as an individual or an organisation.

So it's not so much about answering just one question but instead about considering, planning and answering all three:

- What is your company or product's core capability?
- What is your company or product's unique differentiator?
- What is your company or product's purpose?

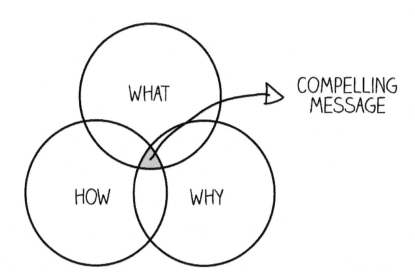

These sound like they might be simple questions to answer, but I can assure you they're not easy. Remember, simple doesn't mean easy. But being clear, concise, and consistent about the answers is incredibly important.

Take a moment in the space below to consider and write out your answers:

What:

_____

How:

_____

Why:

_____

If you can imagine a time where, as an individual, as a team, or as an organisation, you are able to answer these questions clearly and in an articulate manner, then that in itself is extremely powerful. And this is what's known as an Engage Statement.

CUSTOMERS AS ADVOCATES

If you consider the complex buying structures that we now sell into, then to a far greater extent than ever before, we now require our customers to be advocates. More importantly, we have the opportunity to turn our customers into advocates with the language we use to describe what we do, how we're different to the competition, and why someone should work with us.

Within the decision-making unit (the network of interconnected people) customers who act as advocates can accelerate our commercial objective by acting as amplifiers of our message.

The place that we're trying to get to is one where we make it clear what we do, how we're different to the competition, and why somebody should work with us. In doing this well, it's far more likely that our customers will be able to articulate these things too.

Let me flip that around and say it in a different way.

If you aren't clear on what you do, how you're different from the competition, and why someone should work with you, then you can't expect your customers to be clear either.

The structure of an Engage Statement is to clarify what you do specifically, then bridge to 'how' you're different to the competition, before finally describing the 'why' in order to give purpose and meaning, a reason as to why someone should work with you.

Some Examples

What: We're a *training and development organisation* that works *exclusively* within the *medical industry.*

How: We're *by-industry, for-industry* – all of our team have 'carried the bag'.

Why: We combine two principles – *credibility and connection* – to **create modern, dynamic and highly empowered** sales teams.

What: We provide an easy to understand, comprehensive, and cost-effective *wound care range.*

How: We are the only company to offer *independent, university-accredited education to all our customers.*

Why: Everything we do is focused on three critical areas – *innovation, value, and clinical effectiveness.*

What: We're a global manufacturer and supplier of *surgical gloves.*

How: We are the only company to offer *guaranteed supply* **through** *dedicated customer manufacturing.*

Why: We provide *protection* for your most valuable assets – your hands.

Ending your Engage Statement with a question also provides the opportunity to stimulate discussion and guide the conversation. If the person asking the question is in control of the conversation, then by being clear on all of the above and subsequently ending with a question, they provide the chance to make progress through the customer conversation.

The value of an Engage Statement is in bringing clarity and consistency to your message, on being clear on how you're different to the competition, and why someone should work with you.

Be mindful of the difference between simple and easy. Just because this appears simple, it doesn't mean that it's easy. As we've seen, it can provide an incredibly powerful basis for your positioning and future discussions.

ADAPTING YOUR APPROACH

As we've identified, one of the considerations that we need to make when selling into the new economy is that it's no longer about a single decision-maker with a single need or requirement; or that we're able to sell to that person based on them being able to identify solely what they need and us being able to match that with our features and benefits.

We've already described the fact that there are now multiple stakeholders involved in any one sale, and that it's actually a far better description to classify what sales professionals do on a day-to-day basis as managing multiple and complex projects, rather than just being out there trying to make a sale.

Part of the challenge comes in having to deal with multiple types of stakeholder in many different positions, all with varying requirements. The sales professional who can accurately diagnose an individual's preferred style of interaction, their preferred style of communication, and their behaviour and social preferences, will have a significant advantage over his competitors in the market in being able to *Deliver Compelling Messages*.

With this in mind, we're going to explore the idea of adapting a message to different stakeholders, and we're going to explore the idea that comes from being able to identify accurately and then adapt a message based on somebody's communication and behavioural preferences.

VISUAL, AUDITORY, KINESTHETIC (VAK)

We know that all of us have a preferred style in how we communicate with other people, the way that we learn, and the way that we give and receive information. Each of us broadly falls into one of three groups of people in the way that we prefer to communicate.

VISUAL
(SEE IT)

AUDITORY
(HEAR IT)

KINESTHETIC
(DO IT)

The first group are those who are visual learners. That means that they much prefer to receive information and communicate through pictures and images.

That might include reading or it might include watching, and often you will hear these people use language that illustrates the fact that they have a visual preference. If they were to meet you for the first time they might say, 'It's nice to see you', or 'It looks like you're doing well'.

If you were to talk to them about a product, then you might find that, again, somebody with a high visual preference would want to look at that product. They would want to see pictures of it, and they would want to look at illustrations or see a demonstration of how it works.

The next group are those who are auditory learners or who have an auditory preference.

These are people who have a primary preference for the spoken word. Again, if you were to meet them for the first time, or if you were to see them after having not been with them for a while, they may say. 'It's great to hear from you', or they may say, 'It sounds like you're doing well'.

If they were going to use a product for the first time, then they may want to hear about it from you first. They may want to talk through the product in detail or talk through its application or indications specifically.

The third group are those whose primary mode of learning and communicating is known as Kinesthetic; they are people who have a propensity for practical application. Again, if you were to meet such a person in the corridor after having not seen them for a while, they might want to shake your hand, or they might want to give you a hug. They may say, 'It's great to meet you', or they may say, 'It feels like you're doing well',

They will demonstrate a more practical and tactile approach and, therefore, kinesthetic preference. If you were to give them a product they might just want to take it off you, to hold it and give it a go. They will be far less concerned about wanting to read or understand it; instead, they just want to try it.

It is often relatively easy to diagnose these three different preferences from simple conversations, and whilst there are more objective and accurate ways to assess their preferences, just listening to the types of words they use, or the way that they approach a practical situation, is a really useful primary test.

The ability to diagnose these preferences in other people comes from being self-aware and having the ability to diagnose them accurately in yourself.

Give some thought to your own preferences.

Which are you more likely to say?

V - It's great to see you…

A - It's great to hear from you…

K - It's great to meet you…

Which do you feel a greater affinity with?

V – Looking at pictures

A – Listening to sounds

K – Giving things a go

If you knew that somebody was a visual learner, how would that change how you worked with them, or how you described a particular product or scenario to them?

If you knew that somebody was an auditory learner, how would that affect how you engaged with them?

Finally, if you knew that they were a kinesthetic learner, how would that affect how you demonstrated to them?

For visual learners, you would provide them with more pictures and illustrations, more to read, and more videos to look at. You would give them a chance to see a live experience prior to embarking on a first treatment or procedure.

If someone was an auditory learner, you might give them an audio recording, a book, or a podcast to listen to; or you might spend a lot of time talking to them on the telephone or in detail about the product or procedure.

If somebody was a kinesthetic learner then they would be really interested in practical applications, so you would want to do some sort of test, demonstration, or exercise with them.

Imagine the application of this in a group setting.

If you were presenting to a group or a team or board, then without knowing what the differences are in preferred communicational learning styles it would be important to ensure that you adapted your style and your message to include using visual, and auditory, and kinesthetic language and styles, to most effectively communicate your message.

For the visual learners, you might use a PowerPoint slideshow but also flipcharts. For the auditory learners, you might want to give them the opportunity to talk and discuss certain aspects of your particular subject. And for the kinesthetic learners, you might want to give them a chance to do something, perhaps a practical exercise, and to consider how something applies to their business or their organisation.

Understanding and identifying someone as a visual, auditory, or kinesthetic (VAK) learner provides a very simple but very useful method for diagnosing their particular preferences and considering how we might adapt our message to communicate more effectively with them.

BEHAVIORAL STYLES

Another key tool in the assessment of social preferences, and the way you should communicate with people, is known as behavioural styles.

Behavioural Styles is a model that's used to assess interpersonal behaviour. It is based on two variables.

The first is somebody's assertiveness; in other words, his or her likelihood to tell, (which would be high assertiveness) or to ask, (which would be low assertiveness).

As a self-diagnostic, consider the following question.

Do you believe that you're more likely to tell somebody what to do or more likely to ask somebody what to do?

The second variable against which this framework is modelled is based on what's known as responsiveness – and the definition of responsiveness is the degree to which somebody is able to control his or her emotions.

So somebody who has low responsiveness is going to demonstrate a low level of emotion. If somebody is highly responsive, then they are going to demonstrate a high level of emotion.

In other words, assertiveness is the degree to which a person attempts to control or influence a situation or the thoughts or actions of others. Responsiveness is the readiness with which a person outwardly displays emotions or feelings and the manner to which they are able to develop relationships.

So just consider this again as yourself.

Do you believe you are more, or less, likely to show your emotion?

You should now have the answers to the two questions, and we'll come back to what this means in a short while.

By considering a person's behavioural style, we can analyse a number of things that give us clues as to how best to interact with them.

It can allow us to consider their preferred style of communication, and it can also provide us with insights as to how they measure their own personal success. It will give us clues as to how best to support them and how best to present information to them. It will give us an idea about how they approach decision-making, and it will give us a clue as to what we could describe as their specialist function. It also gives us ideas as to how they could behave in conflict or under pressure and what their basic needs are.

In the space below, write down, based on the two questions that you answered, whether you believe you are more or less assertive, or more or less emotional.

Assertiveness: Tell or Ask

_____

Emotional: Control or Show

_____

We can take this information and we can start to plot it.

The basic way to plot this is against a two-by-two framework and you can see on the illustration below how this is done.

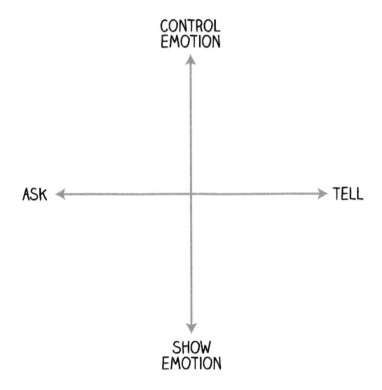

On the Y-axis we have responsiveness and on the X-axis we have assertiveness.

The Y-axis runs from bottom to top. The bottom is about a high outward level of emotion, and the top is about a low outward level of emotion; you can see that the X-axis runs from left to right, with the left-hand side of the axis being low assertiveness and the right-hand side being high assertiveness.

At this point, just put a cross (x) into whichever of these boxes you feel that you currently fall into.

There are different descriptors that sit within each of these boxes.

In the top right-hand box, we have somebody who can be described as a Driver or somebody who is results-orientated, and in the bottom right-hand corner somebody who can be described as an Expressive and is primarily driven by recognition. In the bottom left-hand corner, we have somebody who can be described as Amiable with a focus on relationships and security, and in the top left-hand corner we have somebody who is described as Analytical and is driven by accuracy.

Just look at where you have marked a cross on that page and give some thought as to whether that descriptor accurately describes the type of person that you are.

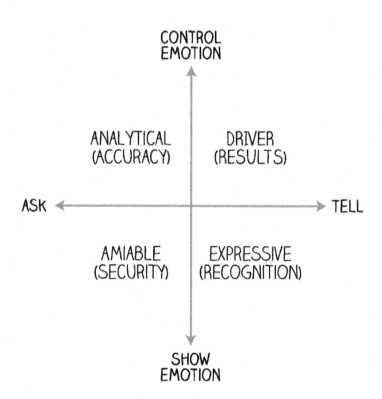

CONTROL
EMOTION

ANALYTICAL
(ACCURACY)

DRIVER
(RESULTS)

ASK

TELL

AMIABLE
(SECURITY)

EXPRESSIVE
(RECOGNITION)

SHOW
EMOTION

A Driver is somebody who is likely to have quick reactions to the here and now and also to sensory input. They care about results, the outcome, and winning.

An Expressive is often thought of as a dreamer and can be quite imaginative. They have a basic need for recognition and the development of their own profile or image. They have a high focus on emotional personal reactions to experiences.

The Amiable is driven by their relationships with others. They care about how others perceive them and, in turn, care about the people they work and interact with. They have a basic need for security.

Finally, the Analytical is logical; they are organised and they tend to analyse situations. They have a basic need for accuracy and would rather be right than win.

The Driver has a basic need to be in control and a basic need to be right; they are focused on the outcome. To solve problems you would need to be assertive and have a number of solutions available for the problem. In full conflict, they can sometimes be aggressive and abrupt.

The Expressive person has a basic need for recognition and in conflict they can be unpredictable and often emotional. In terms of a solution, it's best to allow them to gain composure, to ask questions, and to problem solve.

The Amiable person in conflict is likely to be passive, because they sometimes lack confidence and they will often avoid conflict outright. In terms of a solution, the way to solve conflict with an Amiable person is through reassurance, through support, and by confirming a commitment.

The Analytical person has a basic need to be correct, so it is important to keep to the facts and to listen attentively. In conflict, they can sometimes be negative and they can often procrastinate.

Whilst the best way to assess someone is to complete a full assessment, the most practical approach is to consider these questions: is somebody more or less likely to tell you what to do, or more or less likely to demonstrate emotion?

For the Driver in the top right-hand corner, that person is far more interested in outcomes versus the Analytical person on the left-hand side. Whereas the Analytical person has a need to be right, the Driver has a need for results and outcomes.

An Amiable person is far more interested in relationships than the Expressive person. The Expressive person is far more interested in creativity.

Whilst it's important not to stereotype people against these behavioural styles, it is clearly important to consider the effect that they have on the way you manage your relationships with them. Remember that the core of this is self-awareness. The idea being that the greater the level of self-awareness we have of our own preferences or style, the more likely that we are to notice them in others and, therefore, build better relationships with people than we otherwise would.

Being able to accurately define behavioural styles allows us to get to a point where we can differentiate ourselves from the next person out there.

Remember, there is very little difference between many of the top products. There is often little difference in price as well – a few percent here and a few percent there. What can make a huge difference is the individual salesperson involved in the process.

For many years, companies would look at this problem and be concerned about the salesperson being the point of differentiation, the basic premise being that if they are the primary point of differentiation and they leave us, what happens then? But in the new selling economy, it's far more of a problem for that individual not to be the point of differentiation and stay with an organisation.

What we've explored in this chapter is how we can be the crucial point of differentiation through being able to adapt our message and our behaviour based on somebody's particular preferences. We've considered what those communication preferences might be in terms of learning style (visual, auditory, or kinesthetic) and what they might be in terms of behavioural style.

KEY MESSAGES

- Competitive choice, information available, low tolerance, and lack of time means we have to stand out against the competition

- Being memorable is not just about the language we use, but our tone of voice and non-verbal cues

- Delivering our messages with clarity and uniqueness means we can make an impact, take control of the conversation, and provide a compelling reason to engage

- Many of the greatest wealth creators and change makers in history started with a powerful statement that opened and engaged discussion, started movements, trends, cultures and affected social norms

- There are three questions for which you need clear, concise, and consistent answers:

1. What is your company or product's core capability?

2. What is your company or product's unique differentiator?

3. What is your company or product's purpose?

- The value of an Engage Statement is in bringing clarity, conciseness, and consistency to your message, on being clear about how you're different to the competition, and why someone should work with you.

- In delivering compelling messages, we should be aware of the manner in which people prefer to receive information and interact

- Two specific frameworks to consider are:

  o VAK (Visual, Auditory, and Kinesthetic)

  o Behavioural styles

- Visual communicators prefer to receive information through pictures and images; auditory through sounds, audio, and detail; kinesthetic through doing and practical experience

- Drivers are outcomes-focused and have a basic need for results; Expressives are profile-focused and have a basic need for recognition; Amiables are people-focused and have a basic need for relationships and security; Analyticals are detail-focused and have a basic need for accuracy.

IDENTIFYING CRITICAL ISSUES

We frame our offer from our customer's perspective

WHAT CUSTOMERS WANT

When choices were low and tolerance was high, and when information available was low and time to assimilate the information was higher, then the traditional approach made sense: find out what the customer needed relative to our product's features and benefits, and then satisfy those needs, demonstrating why we had a better product solution than the competition.

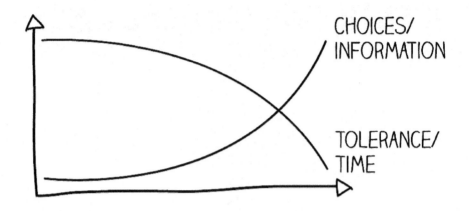

In other words, we pitched the relative features and benefits of product A versus the relative features and benefits of product B.

However, in our changed selling environment, where choices are high and tolerance is low, and when customers are overwhelmed by information with little time to process it, what's the plan?

Unfortunately the notion of asking the customer 'what's important to you?' and then following up with a series of funnelled questions to identify a need before pitching the product's features and benefits versus the competition no longer works.

Here's what a consultant surgeon said recently:

'There's very little now to differentiate the functional performance of most of the top products. What makes a difference is the service we get from the salespeople – and when I say service, I don't just mean making sure we get the right product at the right time, I mean helping us to **think differently** *about how we approach the treatment of our patients.'*

This view isn't an exception but *the expectation*. And it changes everything.

The days of the subservient salesperson (the one described above) or the salesperson who focuses on simply asking the customer for the order is dead. Customers no longer want, expect, or require a salesperson who interviews them as a means to 'identifying a need'. They don't have the tolerance for it, they don't have the time and quite frankly – if that's all they're going to get from their salesperson – they can go online and find for themselves the product that most meets what they believe to be their needs quicker and more effectively. Dinosaurs need to die.

Is this to say that the customer-salesperson relationship is also dead? And is this to say that there is no longer the need for the salesperson? Should we all just call it quits, let the customer order the product online, and then send it in the post?

The answer to all of these questions is an unequivocal 'no'.

The slightly extended answer is, 'no, but...'

Although the relationship is still alive and well (and actually there's a greater need for it than ever before), the manner of the interaction has changed forever.

STANDING OUT FROM THE CROWD

We've discussed the idea of Engage Statements as a way to frame up and differentiate a message that allows you to stand out in a crowd and define what it is that you specifically do, how you are different from the competition, and why someone should work with you.

I want to move on, now, to talk about Critical Issues and with very much the same aim. Critical Issues, like Engage Statements, are a way to engage with a customer around something that we know will make a difference to them. This approach changes the playing field entirely, and it also alters the perception of the salesperson in the customer's mind's eye.

As a result of the way in which these Critical Issues are structured and phrased, the customer sees the salesperson, not as someone who is merely there to elicit information through an interrogation, investigation, or interview, but as somebody who is the *credible expert* within their field, who has a good breadth of understanding about the issues which affect them and, therefore, is able to provoke thought and relevant discussion around an area which is of interest to the customer.

Immediately, that changes the customer's perception of the salesperson – they're not just there in order to have a conversation with only the salesperson's interests in mind. It changes the conversation to frame it from the customer's perspective in a way that allows the salesperson to identify issues which are important and relevant, and then to have a credible discussion around those issues.

The other essential element is that it allows the salesperson to guide that conversation by positioning and identifying (up front) areas of potential interest; then it allows the conversation to flow as a result of those areas of interest.

CRITICAL ISSUES

Critical Issues are areas of specific interest to the customer – goals, objectives, problems, or challenges – that are important, relevant, and objective, and which allow the salesperson to manage the conversation proactively.

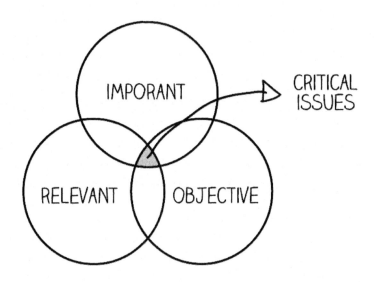

Important means that it's something that, if achieved or changed, would have a significant impact on the customer.

Relevant means that it's something that directly affects them.

And *Objective* means that the discussion is evidenced and allows the salesperson to position himself or herself further as the Credible Expert.

Critical Issues can be identified in three different places when considering a customer:

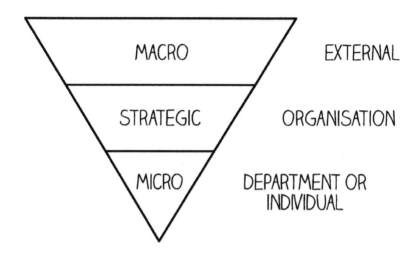

Firstly, they can be identified within what we define as macro challenges.

These are challenges that would affect any customer regardless of their role and regardless of their geographical location. Another way of considering these issues could be as market challenges – they are external factors. In order to define what these macro challenges are, and how we identify them, we need to look at the macroeconomic factors that affect the market. Those factors can be broken down into Political, Economic, Social, Technological, Legal, and Environmental.

Let's consider some of these macroeconomic factors concerning the healthcare market.

An example of a political factor could be Lord Carter's Final Report from February 2016 [13], which was commissioned by the Department of Health and which had political motivation behind it. More generally it might be changes that happen in the run-up to an election, or as a result of a change in government. But those are factors that would affect everybody, regardless of their role and regardless of the specific organisation.

In terms of economic factors, we could acknowledge that in a recent report [14] it was stated that 90% of NHS trusts are running a deficit – a figure up from 5% just three years ago. That's an economic factor which is rather specific but which can affect the entire market. Other economic factors might include austerity measures, or they could be factors linked to trying to reduce the amount of spend on agency staff or changes in VAT. But again, those are economic factors which affect everyone.

Social factors could be things like our increasingly ageing population. Between 2015 and 2020, where the general population is expected to increase by 3%, the numbers of those aged over 65 are likely to increase by 12%. [15] This will place a greater burden on the health service as a result and so these social issues are going to affect everyone.

From a technological point of view, we talked earlier about the fact that today's customers are as well informed as they choose to be because of the internet, but equally, the same can be said for patients. They are now in a position where they will often arrive at a particular hospital or trust having self-diagnosed what they believe the issue to be, together with the type of treatment or product they want. That is a result of changes in technology, and it affects everyone.

From a legal and regulatory point of view, it could include changes to the Medical Devices Directive, or it could include legislation by the Department of Health around requirements for procurement to have migrated to an e-enabled procurement system by March 2017.

And finally, the environmental aspects which would affect all customers might be the requirement to be considerate of carbon footprints, waste reduction, and efficiency improvements.

Exploring these macro factors – these market challenges – provides opportunities for us to identify the Critical Issues which may affect customers.

The second place to look, in order to identify Critical Issues, are within the organisation's strategic objectives.

As with any organisation, a hospital or healthcare institution is no different in that it has a set of values from which it operates. It has a vision, a mission, a set of strategic objectives, and often some tactical deliverables or key priorities. The strategic objectives provide an opportunity to identify initially Critical Issues which may affect that particular customer or that trust.

Often there are four or five things that are included in here, and the amount of information which is readily available on these areas is quite remarkable. Simply by choosing a particular hospital or trust, putting that into a search engine and going to their website, there is masses of information that can be found. It includes annual statements, board minutes and, of course, their published strategic objectives which, as with any organisation (regardless of role and department) everyone within that organisation will be tasked to some degree to help deliver.

In other words, identifying what is particularly important to that trust up front gives us the opportunity to have a credible and thought-provoking discussion.

The third area to identify Critical Issues is within what we call Micro Priorities.

Micro Priorities can be found at a tactical level, within an individual, department, or against the priorities of a strategic objective. Micro Priorities can be found within minutes of board meetings or in annual reports. You might identify them just by having an awareness of what's going on in that particular hospital or trust from the work that you are already doing there, or from the information that you can elicit.

Regardless of which Critical Issue(s) you focus on, three things are important:

1. The issue must be important to the person that you are going to speak to; it must be a problem which needs to be solved, a change that is required, or a goal that they are looking to achieve.

2. Secondly, it has to be relevant to them, so there needs to be some consideration given to the audience and whether or not one particular message is as relevant as the next. It must be something that would make a difference to them.

3. Thirdly, it has to be objective to allow you to demonstrate credibility with the customer. As much as possible, this means that the Critical Issue should be referenced. If it's a macro challenge, then it may be referenced in a published paper or piece of legislation; if it's a strategic Critical Issue then reference the listing on their website or in an annual report, and if it's a key priority, then reference the information that has been published on their website or within the minutes of a board meeting.

THE VALUE WITHIN

Once you've identified a Critical Issue, the next step is to raise that Critical Issue with a customer. The language we use here is again important and deliberate. *'As a result of my research ahead of this meeting, I identified that [raise Critical Issue].'*

When you're stating what you researched and identified, you position yourself with the customer as having a peer-to-peer commercial discussion. Rather than sitting 'across the table' in adversarial style, you metaphorically move your chair beside them and tell them, 'we know this is a Critical Issue for you... let's talk about it'. And this is a very different approach to setting an agenda and using a series of funneled questions to identify a need.

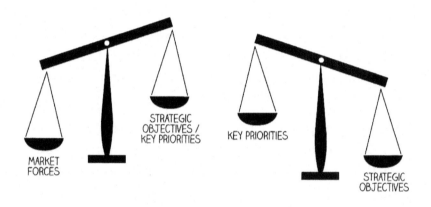

We find that there is often a difficult balance which exists between these Critical Issues. Either between the Market Forces and Strategic Objectives and Key Priorities; or between the Strategic Objectives and Key Priorities.

For example, the healthcare institution that is being driven to reduce costs through reduced funding (Market Forces) on one hand whilst striving to be at the forefront of innovation (Strategic Objective) on the other.

These opposing forces often lead to an imbalance which, in itself, is a Critical Issue. Similarly there may be a drive to improve efficiencies (Strategic Objective) on one hand, whilst being tasked with undertaking more complex work (Key Priority) on the other.

What we've found from the application of this Critical Issues approach is that it creates value, demonstrates your position as the Credible Expert, and ensures that the customer leaves the meeting and discussion with a sense of, 'that was worth my time'.

We know from the research [5] that one of the roles that a customer expects a salesperson to adopt is that of a teacher – in other words, someone who can provide unique insights and knowledge relative to their industry. By identifying these Critical Issues, and ensuring that they are important, relevant, and objective, we match this requirement.

By understanding these Critical Issues across the three customer levels – macro (market), strategic (organizational), and micro (key tactical priorities), you demonstrate that you are the Credible Expert – that you have a good understanding of the factors affecting the customer's world without the need to go through a protracted, scripted, questioning approach to 'identify a need'. The only person who benefits from this outdated approach is the salesperson, and the customer leaves feeling like they've been squeezed for knowledge.

Which leads us nicely to the final point. As much as you should consider your return on investment, whenever you leave a customer or potential customer, they should be doing the same. I would be asking them the same thing. 'Was that worth your time?' By understanding and articulating these issues and then framing the discussion from their perspective, you increase the chances of this being a positive return on investment for the customer as well as you.

KEY MESSAGES

- There's now very little to differentiate the functional performance of most top products
- As a result, customers want salespeople who can help them to think differently
- Critical Issues are areas of interest that are important, relevant, and objective
- They can be found in three areas of challenge:
    1. Macro (market)
    2. Strategic (objectives)
    3. Micro (priorities)
- Being able to identify and highlight Critical Issues provides further opportunity to position yourself as a Credible Expert with customers
- It offers the chance to take control of, and drive, the customer discussion, framed from their perspective
- As a result, customers find far more value from a Critical Issues-based approach than traditional funneled sales approaches

PROVOKING THOUGHT AND DISCUSSION

Provoking thought creates a powerful dynamic for change

CURRENT AND FUTURE STATES

Of course, it's one thing to identify and raise the Critical Issue, and something else entirely to have a meaningful conversation around it. But if we accept the premise that by doing so we frame the discussion from the customer's perspective, then we're already taking strides towards a discussion that has the capacity to affect change.

Once the Critical Issue has been identified, the next step is to be able to raise it with the customer and to raise it in a way that provokes discussion. We do that by identifying the Critical Issue, highlighting it with them, and then using a question to provoke considered discussion about their Current and Future States.

This gives rise to the salesperson taking on the role of the coach as they work to understand where the customer is today, and where they hope to be in the future.

A customer's Current State is where they are today with regards to their Threats, Opportunities, Weaknesses, and Strengths (TOWS) and requires us to appeal to their rational and emotional considerations.

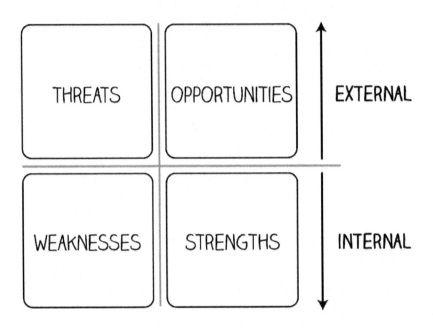

These rational considerations result from asking about the impact of the Critical Issue on place, products, or processes – the emotional considerations result from asking about people, purpose, or pride.

Think about this for a moment from your own perspective. If I ask you to describe your last holiday to me in terms of the place (the hotel, resort, location), the products (the way the holiday was assembled, flights, transfers, hotels) or the process (how you booked it, online, call centre, agent) then I'll get a lot of valuable information and specific detail.

If I ask you to describe the people you went with or met (boyfriend, girlfriend, partner, family or friends), the sense of purpose it created (what it meant to you, why you went, how significant it was) or the pride you felt (what the most satisfying element was, and what happiness it provoked) then we'll get a very different account of events and ones which tell me far more about you and what's important to you.

Let's consider each in turn:

Rational Considerations

- Place – the location(s), organisation(s), or department(s) that impact the operation

- Products – the products, services, or solutions that affect the overall operation

- Processes – the constituent elements that, when combined, contribute to the operation

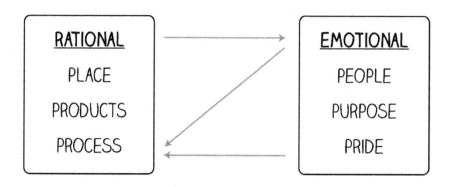

Emotional Considerations

- People – the effect that any Critical Issue has with regard to the people within the organisation
- Purpose – the significance that this issue has, or the meaning it holds for them
- Pride – the degree to which people are pleased and/or satisfied personally

The questions that provoke the most insightful discussion are the Four Lens questions and include:

- Reverse Lens
- Telescopic Lens
- Wide Lens
- Third-Eye Lens

Before we look at each of these in a little more detail, it is essential to note here that, unlike older approaches to questioning, this isn't about open or closed questions, nor about funneling questions, but about provoking thought and discussion. That's it. We want to provoke discussion around these rational and emotional areas so that customers think differently. If they can think differently, we can change behaviour and with it, results.

But don't get too focused on the result – that's the outcome, the consequence of doing the other things right; of creating value by provoking thought and discussion about the customer's Current and Future States.

Where are they today and where might they be in the future.

THE FOUR LENSES

The Reverse Lens allows you to ask the question in a way that provides the customer with the opportunity to look at the situation from another person's perspective.

- *How would the other person involved in the situation view this?*
- *How do their [goals, objectives, or priorities] impact you?*
- *How do your [goals, objectives, or priorities] impact them?*

This is an extremely useful approach if you are having any type of disagreement or conflict with someone else or if they are unable to see another person's perspective. In our world of multiple stakeholders, complex decision-making units, and multi-disciplinary teams, this is often our role. Take time to see the situation from their perspective. What are they seeing that you aren't? What can they see which is influencing the way they think?

The Telescopic Lens helps you provide the customer with the opportunity to take a longer-term view of the situation, to get some distance on the issue, either into the past or the future.

- *How would you view this situation in 12 months' time?*
- *What progress have you made over the last 12 months?*
- *In 12 months' time, how will you know if you've been successful?*

This can be particularly helpful if things haven't gone well, for whatever reason, or for getting customers to consider the actions that have brought them up to the present day. Taking a long-term view can help put things into context and allow them to picture a future working with you. This can be a great approach during idea generation or planning sessions. What will things look like in 12 months and how could you capitalise on them?

The Wide Lens allows you to help a customer to broaden their thinking, to be open minded, to think in terms of possibilities and generate ideas. Remember that *those who consider greater possibilities create increased opportunities.*

- *What options haven't you considered yet?*
- *What else might you possibly consider?*
- *Who else might possibly be interested in a project like this?*

This sort of questioning helps when you're feeling at a dead-end, when you're out of ideas, when you don't know what to try next. Don't limit your thinking; instead, use this type of question to free yourself and others.

The Third-Eye Lens provides you with the opportunity to gain additional objectivity from someone removed from the situation. This could be a person, a place, or a publication.

- *A prominent [person] suggests this particular approach. What is your assessment of that?*

- *An acknowledged [place] has recently advocated the use of this product or service. What consideration have you given to it?*

- *A recent [publication] indicated the importance of benchmarking best practice. What areas of improvement have you highlighted?*

You can use this lens and these questions with anyone, including yourself, and they can provide some much-needed objectivity. By framing the discussion from a person, place, or publication, you remove the subjectivity. You remove the notion that it's you versus them. 'Here's what this [person, place, or publication] suggests. What do you think?'

The Four Lenses are a tool, but here again, we see that the key to this is asking great questions – questions that provide a different perspective and questions that remove barriers. Forget open and closed questions. Instead, focus on asking great questions. By getting people to change their perspective on the situation, you provide a different set of options. As such, we're looking for questions that are genuinely curious, explore risks and consequences, explore effects and benefits, and which survey away (negative) and towards (positive) motivators of change. Our acronym for these questions is GREAT.

Great questions should be GREAT questions; questions that:

G   Show GENUINE curiosity

R   Explore RISKS and consequences

E   Explore positive EFFECTS and benefits

A   Explore 'AWAY from motivation'

T   Explore 'TOWARDS motivation'

Keep in mind that the goal is to provoke thought and discussion, to challenge assumptions, and to ensure that the customer thinks differently.

YOUR ROLE AS A COACH

By combining the Critical Issue that you've identified with a Four Lens question, we have the opportunity to provoke thought and discussion around issues that we know to be important and relevant to the customer. In other words, we frame the discussion from the customer's perspective and demonstrate our credibility.

What we're aiming to do over the course of the discussion is the same as any great coach. And if you've had the opportunity to work with a coach, you'll be very familiar with this.

That is, to have the customer describe their Current and Future States. In other words, with regards to the Critical Issue, where are they today and where they want to be at some point in the future.

We know that customers want salespeople who can help them achieve their objectives, help them to avoid risks, mistakes, errors, and pitfalls. This is the role of a Coach and a role that needs to be adopted with customers.

So rather than being in a position where we are relying on them to tell us about a need or requirement through a series of funneled questions, we are able to change the nature of the conversation to one which rests on us being responsible for provoking discussion and then framing it much more from the customer's perspective.

As a result of that, we are again seen as Credible Experts in our field.

TWO CONVERSATIONS

I want to describe two conversations that exemplify the points above, and the value and importance that these Critical Issue questions can play.

The first example is with a salesperson who had been on territory for around 12 months. They had secured a meeting with a Senior Category Buyer at a large teaching hospital in the South of the UK.

We had gone along to this particular meeting to meet the Senior Category Buyer and unbeknown to the salesperson, they had also brought along their Procurement Manager. So this, on the face of it, was a great opportunity.

The salesperson sat down to begin the meeting and opened the meeting as you would ordinarily expect someone to open a meeting. After some initial small talk, the salesperson asked the Procurement Manager and the Senior Category Buyer the following question:

'What's the most important thing to you?'

Now, at this moment, I want to just pause and let you consider what the answer to that question was from the two procurement people sitting in a UK hospital.

Of course, the answer that came back was 'Price, cost, we want to save money'.

At this moment in time, the salesperson was understandably on the back foot and he then proceeded to open up his product catalogue, flipped to one of the middle pages, and asked the procurement team, 'Whose equivalent of this product do you currently use in theatre?'

The Procurement Manager said 'I don't know, we don't have that information available. We hold 27,000 lines of stock in our theatres so I don't specifically know which one of those we use'.

'Oh,' said the salesperson, 'You wouldn't happen to know how much the one is that you use, do you?'

'Well, no, of course not. I don't know that information, but more to the point, don't you know?' exclaimed the Procurement Manager.

Again, the salesperson was on the back foot. For what seemed like the next five or six minutes he continued this cycle of identifying products, asking which equivalents were used, and asking for price information.

In the end the Procurement Manager brought the meeting to a close and said 'You know, I think the best thing for us to do, the best thing for you to do is, if you send me a copy of your catalogue and a copy of your price list, then we'll spend some time going through it and see what we use versus what you have and reconcile that with your price list. If we can save any money, then we'll get back in touch with you'.

With that they stood up from the table and walked back to their offices.

Now contrast this with the second procurement meeting:

A salesperson with a similar tenure on territory walked into a very similar scenario. This time it's a large teaching hospital in the North West of the UK.

As the salesperson walked into the meeting, again he was met with a Senior Buyer and a Procurement Manager. The Procurement Manager said to the salesperson 'I'm really pleased that you have come today', and with that he dropped onto the table an A4 lever arch folder full of invoices. He said 'I'm really pleased you came today because I wanted to go through each of these invoices, line by line, and look to see where we can save some money and where we can save on some carriage charges'.

At this point the salesperson paused and said, 'We can certainly look at that as I know that you've got a key objective for the rest of this year to save 5% on non-pay spend. One of the things which I had identified in my research ahead of this meeting with you, was that the Trust had recently spent £1.3 million on a piece of capital equipment for theatre and as I saw that, I considered the challenge that you, as procurement have and the difficult balance which you try to manage between continuing to reduce the deficit and managing a budget, whilst all the while trying to ensure that the hospital remains at the forefront of technology and innovation and also ensuring a positive public profile for the Trust within the local area. I was really interested to get your thoughts on that balance and that challenge. So perhaps you can spend a little time talking to me about that, and how you've tried to manage that balance over the last 12 months and what your plans are for the next 12 months?'.

For the next 30 minutes we sat and listened to the Procurement Manager and a Senior Buyer describe a number of the challenges which they faced in trying to reduce the deficit whilst all the while maintaining a positive public profile and continuing to be ahead in terms of technology and innovation.

We explored a number of areas of interest to them and at the end of the meeting the Procurement Manager said, 'You know, I'm sorry we don't have any more time to continue the discussion and also I'm aware that we didn't get to talk through these invoices and all the carriage charges, but perhaps we can schedule another meeting together. Before you go, there is somebody else who I think you would be interested to talk to, because we recently appointed a new General Manager and I think that they would value a discussion with you too'.

So that meeting was left with another meeting in the diary for Procurement and a meeting booked as a referral with a newly appointed General Manager.

Now there's nothing clever, sophisticated, or fancy about the differences in these two conversations or the approach.

Both were relatively inexperienced salespeople with similar tenure in their role.

It's just that the first example relied on the salesperson to ask a series of funneled questions, asking, 'What's the most important thing to you?' en route to trying to identify a need; whereas in the second conversation, there is a salesperson as a Credible Expert in their field, as somebody who has researched the organisation, who's identified a Critical Issue, and who has raised that with a key customer in order to have a thought-provoking, credible, important, and relevant discussion.

As you think about those two conversations, think about which one of them is more likely to lead to a successful and positive outcome.

The first one is an example of what I would call 'old world' or 'traditional' selling.

The latter is an example of what is required to sell and be successful in today's modern selling environment; it's an example of a Credible Expert who can identify Critical Issues and questions about Current and Future States.

As you think about that, just consider the steps that we've discussed so far:

1. To identify a Critical Issue which affects that particular customer or trust.

    a. Those Critical Issues need to be researched, need to be credible, important, and relevant, and visible in three areas:

        i. Macro – things which affect everyone. The market or macroeconomic factors.

        ii. Strategic – things which are present in the organisation's strategic objectives

        iii. Micro – things which can be seen in the key priorities of the organisation, the daily tactical activities that individuals and departments are focused on.

2. Once those factors have been identified through research, they need to be raised to a customer along with the question – a Four Lens question – to provoke thought and discussion.

Now at this point, I just want to pause, and raise something that was asked of me recently.

I was asked, *"Should we try to link that Critical Issue to our product or service, or our solution?"*

We're going to explore the answer (and methodology behind the answer) to this question in a moment. Before that, however, I just want you to consider the difference in those two procurement conversations.

Because if you think that this conversation is about making a quick sale, then you're missing the point.

In the second conversation, the discussion never moved to the company's product, service, or solution. It was a conversation about the customer and the things that are important to them. It was a conversation that was framed from the customer's perspective and it was a conversation that was congruent with the customer's world.

Simply by being able to have that type of discussion, it puts you ahead of the majority.

That type of discussion was an incredibly important and relevant discussion about a Critical Issue, which you've identified, raised, and discussed – differentiating you from the competition.

So if you do nothing else at this point, the customer sees you as a Credible Expert in your field.

Do you want to be thought of as a sales rep? Somebody who is there to ask a series of funneled questions, to elicit information in order to identify a need, and then push your features and benefits?

Or do you want to be seen as a Credible Expert in your field? Someone who is able to relate to the customer's world, who is able to have a thought-provoking discussion as somebody who sees things from the customer's perspective.

THE FOUR DRIVERS OF CUSTOMER CHANGE

By exploring Current and Future States, something interesting happens. As a result of the customer describing where they are today, versus where they might be at some point in the future, we gain an insight into the Driver(s) Of Customer Change.

These drivers are broken down into four areas:

- Productivity
- Performance
- Profile
- Purse

Productivity is related to quantity or output. For example, 'we want to do more treatments', or 'complete more cases on a list', or 'improve our overall efficiency'.

Performance is related to the result or the outcome. Clues you might hear include, 'we want to improve patient outcomes', or 'we want to increase post-operative range of movement', or 'we want to get patients mobile on the same day as their procedure'.

Profile is linked to image. If this is the driver of change, you might pick up language such as, 'we want to be recognised for our work', or 'the impact of the recent report is something we need to focus on', or 'how our patients view us is the only thing that matters'.

And Purse is related to income, costs, and profitability. Here you'll hear people say things like, 'we need to increase revenue into the practice', or 'it's our cost base that we need to reduce', or 'we're still a business and we need to ensure that we are profitable'.

By listening out for the language and the links to each of the four drivers above, we can consider what the key driver of change really is. Why are they prepared (or not) to take the proposed action?

Once we've identified where the Gap exists and what the primary driver is, we can then describe how we've helped a similar customer in a similar position, further demonstrating our value as the Credible Expert, as we begin to facilitate change.

KEY MESSAGES

- Once we've identified Critical Issues, we use a range of questions in order to provoke thought and discussion.

- These questions are Four Lens questions:

  1. Reverse Lens

  2. Telescopic Lens

  3. Wide Lens

  4. Third-eye Lens

- We want to provoke discussion so that customers think differently. If they can think differently, we can change behaviour and with it, results

- In doing so, we further position ourselves as the Credible Expert

- We ask GREAT questions to explore Current and Future States

- As a result of the customer describing where they are today, versus where they might be at some point in the future, we glean an insight into the Drivers Of Customer Change of which there are four:

1. Productivity (or output)

2. Performance (or outcome)

3. Profile (or image)

4. Purse (or financial)

- We can then identify a Gap that allows us to demonstrate how we've helped similar customers in a similar position

SHARING EXPERIENCE INSIGHTS

The stories we tell transform what a customer believes is possible

CURRENT AND FUTURE STATES

THE VALUE OF STORIES

The word story is derived from the Greek word meaning knowing, knowledge, and wisdom. For thousands of years, stories have been used to entertain, teach, pass on wisdom, record history, represent beliefs, explore new ideas, share experiences, build community, and express creativity.

It is the basic unit of learning and, as such, plays a key role in our development from our earliest years.

When we listen to a story, it gives us the opportunity to create our own images, our own personal blend of imagined sights, sounds, and feelings, and consider a different perspective. And importantly, facts wrapped in stories are 22 times more memorable than facts are alone [16].

In our recent research, across a range of medical companies, it was found that the majority of salespeople, when asked, weren't able to articulate what they or their company do without describing product features and benefits.

Just consider that for a moment: *the majority of people out there can't describe what they do in a compelling way that will resonate with a range of customer types.*

But it's understandable, if not acceptable, that this is the case. After all, many of us have been conditioned to talk about the features and benefits of a product in the hope that one of them might stick like glue.

If we say enough, perhaps the customer will relate to one of them, and we're off and running.

But there are two main problems we now face that means that this approach is unsuitable:

1. Our decision-making units (and therefore our customers) are broader than ever before with a range of requirements that fit outside the standard features and benefits of our product

2. Many of those decision-makers (those people with high power) are removed from the end-user and do not care about the functional performance of the product because of the equity which exists in the market between most products

As a result of this, we need to find a way to shift the dialogue from being product-centred and purely logical, to one that is commercially-orientated, rational, emotive, and linked to Critical Issues, so that we can demonstrate how we've helped similar customers in similar positions. In doing so, we further position ourselves as the Credible Expert.

THE IMPORTANCE OF CERTAINTY

The truth is that most people don't like to be the first.

The 'diffusion of innovation' curve [17] shown below confirms that only 2.5% of people are innovators; those who are willing to deal with a high degree of uncertainty and who often have the resources to soften any risk. Even the Early Adopters only account for the next 13.5%. They are the people willing to take on a perceived leadership role as the change agents of the future. The early and late majority account for 34% and even the laggards, those most resistant to change, account for 16%. So in real terms, it's more likely that you will come up against a laggard than you would an early adopter.

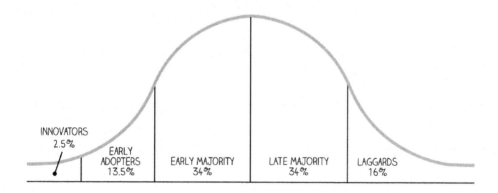

What does this tell us? This tells us that people like certainty. They like to know that there have been others there before them, others willing to take the risk; others who put themselves out there and test the water.

So part of our role is to facilitate the connection with others – physically (in person) or mentally (through our experiences) to ensure that customers feel a sense of certainty. It means that they can take comfort from the reference and testimonial of 'a similar customer in a similar position to them', someone you have worked with and who has been successful as a result of that work.

Notice the language, 'similar customer in a similar position', as it's quite important. 'Similar customer' resonates with them because it's not someone bigger or smaller, which may create a negative perception. 'Similar position' resonates because it's not someone who they cannot relate to. It's about making our stories relevant.

This way, we can then help customers to see, hear, and feel certainty.

PICTURING THE FUTURE

Why would you go to a DIY store and buy a drill?

People in general struggle to picture the future.

Ask someone why they want to buy a drill and they'll probably tell you it's because they want to drill a hole. But that's not the real reason they want the drill.

They want it so that they can put up the shelves in their children's room; they want it to put up the family pictures from last Christmas; or they want it so that they can fit that new 42" television that they've been looking forward to sitting and watching with their partner.

People don't want the hole. They want the experience.

People don't want the product. They want the experience.

And people don't want the service. They want the experience.

But the logical part of the brain doesn't default to the experience, and so it's our job, as salespeople, to help them picture the future by providing them with stories and testimonials of how we've helped similar people in similar positions – to help them experience what working with us looks, sounds, and feels like.

These stories, these experiences, testimonials, and insights, give us the chance to create images of relatable experience. They create a buying (and future) vision of what the world could look like, help us to objectify our experience, allow us to demonstrate credibility, and ultimately provide the platform from which to link our Unique Offer to the customer's key drivers of change.

FACILITATING THROUGH EXPERIENCE INSIGHTS

The stories that help customers gain certainty of what working with us might feel like, and which help them to picture the future, are called Experience Insights.

They help raise awareness to a different perspective that leads to a possible next action or step, and that leads to the opportunity for progressive or helpful thinking towards our product or service. And they help others *experience* how you've helped others to achieve their key driver of change, whether that be productivity, performance, profile, or purse.

Once we've identified both the Gap and the customer driver, we have the opportunity to demonstrate our experience as a credible expert in how we've solved similar problems before. We do that through the use of stories, which offer the customer the opportunity to arrive at insights about ways of working which they hadn't previously considered.

It's not enough simply to assume that the customer understands how we've helped similar customers in a similar position. Instead, we need to demonstrate our credibility as an expert in the field by going a lot deeper and being a lot more specific. We can do this in three ways:

- Based on our own personal experience, relating those times when we've personally helped similar customers in a similar position

- By talking about what the business or the company has done to help similar customers in a similar position

- With reference to what others outside the organisation (other peers or likeminded individuals) have done to help similar customers in a similar position

CONTEXT
AIM
SPECIFIC STEPS
EVIDENCE OF RESULTS

Consider the great stories you hear. They have two things: an essence and a structure. The essence is that they are engaging, dynamic, relatable, and emotive.

The structure that we need to use in order to deliver that experience, and therefore provoke the insight of what is possible with the customer, is to adopt the following CASE approach, Context, Aim, Specific Steps and Evidence of the End Result:

- To identify or to provide examples of the situation or the **Context** that relates to the Critical Issue

- To define the **Aim** or the overarching objective

- To explain the **Specific Steps** or activities that were undertaken

- To provide **Evidence** of the **End Result**

It's no use being too general and just telling a customer, 'hey, don't worry, I've completed a successful evaluation before – I know what I'm doing!' It would just be too weak or too un-substantive. What we need is essence and structure.

By applying the CASE approach, we're able to provide a deeper context and clarity on what we did.

In a similar hospital to yours, we worked to help them improve their overall operating efficiencies. (This is the Context.) We worked to convert 14 theatres from their incumbent product over to their chosen product. (This is the Aim.) Over the course of a six-week period, we were on site to manually switch over the products, established a competency-based training programme, and provided on-call customer support to ensure a smooth transition. (These are the Specific Steps.) This resulted in 100% completion of our education programme, a 95% customer satisfaction score, and an immediate 25% reduction in cost. (These are the Evidence of End results).

In a similar practice to yours, we helped them to improve patient footfall within a shopping centre. (This is the Context.) We worked to increase the number of prospective patients entering the clinic by 20% over a four-week period. (This is the Aim.) We focused on three main areas: local marketing, advertising within the centre, and a specific promotion for new patients. We provided a script for a local radio advert, posters and banners for the centre, and staff to assist with the promotion (These are the Specific Steps.) Over the four week period, we had new patient enquiries up by 37%, added 500 people to our mailing list, and have booked another promotion for the following quarter.

That would be a far clearer and better-structured way of providing that experience. We have the essence of an engaging story, along with a structure that provides the context, aim, specific steps, and evidence of the end result.

By telling stories, we can ensure that we relate our relevant experience to customers in a way that resonates with them. Remember that the majority of people out there can't describe what they do without detailing features and benefits. For the most part, that approach will not resonate with the broader and deeper spectrum of customer we now need to engage with.

The CASE approach gives us a structure to describe similar experiences with similar customers in a way that lets them know that *we can help them*. It provides them with certainty of what it might be like to work with us, and it gives us the chance to help them picture the future. In doing so, we are able to transform what customers believe is possible.

So, we've identified and highlighted a Critical Issue, and discussed Current and Future States to provoke thought and discussion. We've identified the key drivers of customer change, and we've demonstrated our credibility by describing how we helped a similar customer in a similar position through an Experience Insight. And so, finally, we have the opportunity to describe how we can help them and articulate our unique offering.

KEY MESSAGES

- Most people, when asked, can't articulate what they do without describing the features and benefits of the product

- This creates a problem because of the breadth and depth of the decision-making unit we sell into, where the details of the product become less important

- In order to mitigate this problem, we have to learn to create stories which position us as the Credible Expert and focus on what we've done and the outcomes that we've produced

- Customers like certainty and they need help to picture the future

- The word '*story*' is derived from the Greek word meaning knowing, knowledge, and wisdom

- By sharing our experience stories, we provide a testimonial of how we've helped similar customers in similar positions

- We can talk about our own personal experiences, that of our team, or that of others

- These Experience Insights should retain the engaging essence of successful stories whilst following a proven structure to ensure maximum impact:

  o The **Context** which relates to the Critical Issue

  o The **Aim** or the overarching objective

  o The **Specific Steps** or activities that were undertaken

  o The **Evidence** of the **End Result**

- This structure is known as the CASE Structure

DEMONSTRATING YOUR UNIQUE OFFERING

DEMONSTRATING
UNIQUE
OFFERING

Our offer becomes compelling when we create the desire for change

KEEP THE PRODUCT IN THE BAG

If I think back to my time learning to sell, there was one tactic that we were always told to rely on. 'Get the product out of the bag'.

This ended up being the default position – if in doubt, get the product out; if you don't know what to do next, get the product out; if you felt like the meeting was drifting away, get the product out. In fact, you know what, just get the product out of the bag!

This can be a particular problem when you genuinely believe in the product. There's an innate desire to enthusiastically talk about, and demonstrate, the product as quickly as possible. But by getting the product out too early in the discussion, a number of things happen:

1. It becomes a pitch of one product versus the next

2. It changes the focus of the discussion from one framed from the customer's perspective to one based on your product

3. It doesn't allow any tension or desire to be created in the conversation with your customer because they already know that your answer is always going to be 'the product'

We know that to be successful in the new selling environment, it's no longer about the features and benefits of one product versus the features and benefits of the next. We also know that the conversation needs to be framed from the customer's perspective and we do that through the use of Critical Issues. And by doing this, and using the structure we've described to manage the customer conversation, we create a tension and desire over the course of the discussion.

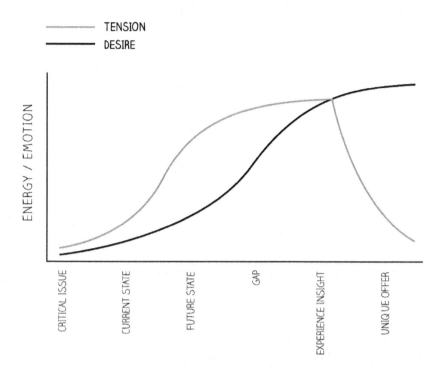

TENSION
DESIRE

ENERGY / EMOTION

CRITICAL ISSUE

CURRENT STATE

FUTURE STATE

GAP

EXPERIENCE INSIGHT

UNIQUE OFFER

If you consider the illustration above, we have two lines (and two states) which are being created. The first is tension and the second is desire. Desire lags behind tension through the initial phases of the discussion.

By raising a Critical Issue with a customer, we immediately begin to build a state of tension between the Current State and future state. As we move through these steps, that tension starts to build as the customer realises that there is a Gap between where they are today and where they might be in the future. As this tension rises, so does the desire to do something about it. Psychologists refer to this tension as cognitive dissonance, and this dissonance – or tension – continues to increase through to the point where you describe your Experience Story and tell them, 'but don't worry, we've helped a similar customer in a similar position'.

At that moment, the tension in the discussion dissipates whilst the desire to want to do something about it continues to rise. So that finally, as you present your Unique Offering, you've created the desire for change so that your offer is a compelling one.

This is what a Procurement Manager said after a recent sales meeting: *'It became clear that we needed to make a change; that something needed to happen. I felt that the salesperson could help and I was willing then to be told how. By the time they did, I was ready and willing to commit to the next step'*.

If the product is introduced too early in the discussion, before the Critical Issue has been identified, before the Current and Future States have been explored (through thought and discussion), and before you've shown how you've helped a similar customer in a similar position, then the desire to change is never fully created. The foundation for change isn't fully developed.

So resist the temptation to get the product out too early in the discussion. Because our offer only becomes compelling once we've created the desire for change.

DRIVING THE CUSTOMER CONVERSATION

The processes that we've outlined in the previous chapters and the steps involved: Selecting The Right Customer, Delivering Compelling Messages, Identifying Critical Issues, Provoking Discussion, and Sharing Experience Insights, are designed to provide a structure for thought and discussion.

More than that, they allow you to take control and guide the customer conversation. There are a number of benefits to doing this:

1. You position the conversation based on a Critical Issue and therefore frame it from the customer's perspective

2. As the person asking the questions, you are in control of the conversation

3. The discussion on price is one that you are in control of, and can raise at the time that best suits the conversation

STACKING THE VALUE

By following the Critical Issue approach, by positioning the conversation from the customer's perspective, and by guiding a thought-provoking discussion, it allows you to do what's called 'stacking the value'.

Stacking the value is a way of demonstrating the value that you, and your organisation's product or service, can provide so that the perceived value in working with you continues to rise above the associated investment.

Value can be in the practical activities that you undertake but can also be in the way you make customers think – the thoughts and discussion you provoke during the course of the customer conversation. Both contribute to stacking the value and allow you to position yourself as the credible expert.

One of the most common questions I hear is, 'what's the best way to deal with price?' And it's interesting because an objection around price is a clear demonstration that two things have happened. Firstly, that price has been raised too early in the discussion. And secondly, that the customer does not perceive enough value in the product or service to meet their minimum level of investment.

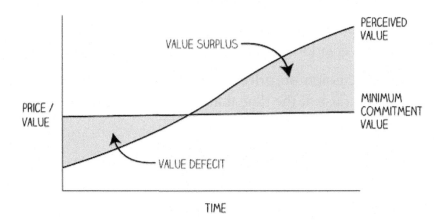

Price becomes far less of an objection once the desire to change has been created through the customer journey that we've described. Price becomes far less of an issue when the customer acknowledges that there is a dissonance between where they are today and where they might be in the future. And price becomes far less of an issue when the customer understands that you've helped others in a similar position.

Price becomes an issue for customers when they perceive the cost of the product to be higher than the value associated with it. In order to alleviate this pressure and risk, we have to both give and demonstrate value over the course of the customer conversation. We do this by effectively articulating the reason(s) why someone should work with us, positioning ourselves as the credible expert, showing how we've helped similar customers in a similar position, and creating the desire for change.

We spoke earlier about the key drivers of customer change (productivity, performance, profile, purse) and how those are identified as a result of exploring the Current and Future States of the customer.

What we find is that these drivers link directly back to the Critical Issue.

It's essential that we identify and understand this because it's the real reason why the customer would consider adopting your product or service.

With very little to differentiate most of the top products, the truth is that it's less and less likely that customers are willing to make a change because of the product itself. It's far more likely that they are willing to change because of what else they get through the use of the product, both in terms of service and support as well as the manner and extent to which it links back to their Critical Issue.

THE THREE PRODUCT LEVELS

With this in mind, it's important to acknowledge that the products and services we sell are not one-dimensional but exist at three levels. Understanding the three levels that your product or service operates at, and being able to articulate them confidently, allows you not only to deliver more compelling messages but ensures that you speak to the different requirements of the customer.

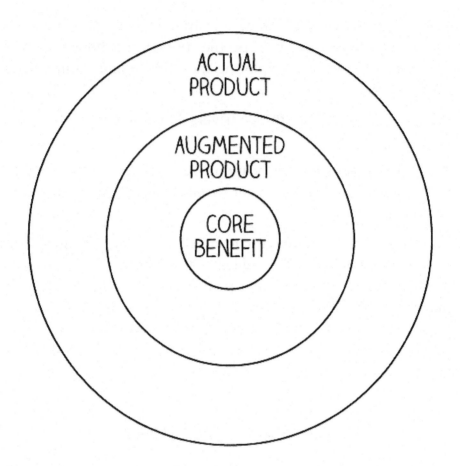

The first is the Actual Product, which is the tangible product or service. It includes things such as the features, design, packaging, and the brand.

The second level is the Augmented Product and includes the delivery, support, service, warranty, and finally, implementation.

The third level is the Core Benefit, and this addresses the question, *'What is the buyer really buying?'* It is the part of the product that bridges the Gap between their Current and Future States and usually relates directly to the Critical Issue. If the

Critical Issue, or Gap, which has been identified is improving capacity, then that core benefit should link directly back to that Gap of increasing capacity.

Below are some examples of each of the three different product levels:

Actual

- *A range of wound closure products*
- *A cost-effective portfolio of IV access products*
- *Laparoscopic stapling equipment*
- *The largest range of surgical dressings*
- *Absorbable theatre drapes*
- *Water-resistant surgical gowns*
- *Clear removable aligners*

Augmented

- *24 hours/7 day customer service*
- *University-accredited / educated*
- *Next day delivery*
- *E-Enabled ordering and invoicing*
- *Competency-based training*
- *Annual audit and review*
- *In-service training*
- *Multiple order and delivery routes*
- *Practice and clinic development*

Core

- *Improved operating room efficiency*

- *Reduced length of stay*

- *Reduced surgical site infection*

- *Improved clinical outcomes*

- *Enhanced public perception*

- *Clinical research publication*

- *Reduced waste*

- *Reduced processing costs*

- *Increased patient footfall*

Identifying the Core Benefit and being able to articulate it is crucial in effectively demonstrating your Unique Offering. And because that Critical Issue and the Gap that exists between Current and Future States is different depending on the customer, then your offer and the message that you shape around it should also be unique to that specific customer.

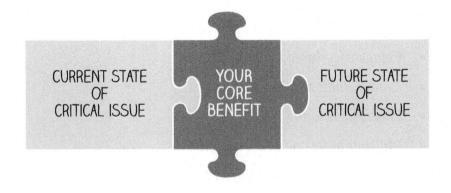

So, in order to link back from our Unique Offering, we should be absolutely clear about what the Core Benefit is and how that associates with the Critical Issue. We should also clearly state the augmented and actual product.

By following this structure, we are able to discuss with the customer not just a compelling reason why they should spend time with us, but also explore issues, themes, and topics that are important and relevant to them. Then we can use the structure which we've just described to link that back through Current and Future States, through the Gap, through our experience, and finally to our solution.

As a result, we flip the traditional model of selling on its head so that, rather than using a series of funneled questions to identify need, we demonstrate our credibility as an expert in our field by identifying the Critical Issues that we know are important and relevant to customers.

These are: exploring their impact, exploring Current and Future States, identifying the requirements, the Gap, and then finally linking that through our experience to our core product, augmented product, and core benefit.

KEY MESSAGES

- By following the approach outlined, there are four main benefits:
  1. We position the conversation based on a Critical Issue and therefore frame it from the customer's perspective
  2. As the person asking the questions, we are in control of the conversation

3. The discussion on price is one that we are in control of, and which we can raise at a time that best suits the discussion

4. Most importantly, we position ourselves as the Credible Expert with our customers and gain the opportunity to Stack Value

- There are three levels at which the product can be communicated:

  o Actual. Augmented. Core.

PART 3 – BECOMING THE CREDIBLE EXPERT

The changed dynamics in the selling environment create a window of opportunity for the salesperson who can adopt the role of the professional change maker and project manager. The salesperson who can focus first on creating value for the customer, as a teacher, a coach, and a facilitator, is the one who will stand out in a crowded market, outperform the competition, and position themselves as the Credible Expert.

CREATING VALUE AND SIGNIFICANCE

Our results are directly proportional to the value we create for our customers

THE ONLY WAY

Do customers really care about a small technical change that, in reality, isn't going to make a huge difference to the performance that they experience, or the outcome that they achieve?

No, of course not.

The only way to be successful in the new selling economy is to create value for our customers first. And so one of the biggest challenges here is moving beyond the idea of 'creating value' as a buzz word to real, practical action. As the Credible Expert, it is your primary role to find ways to create value for your customers first, frequently, and without expectation.

Although this final element comes towards the end of our discussion, it is certainly not a terminal step. It is the common message and the default state throughout: create value and significance.

THE NECESSITY OF VALUE

There was a point in time when it was really only the company who was seen by the customer as the significant source of information; an entity the customer would approach in order to get the knowledge that they needed. And so the customer would only be as well informed as the company allowed them to be.

They would often rely on the company's representative to see whether there were any new advances or any changes in products, and they would be at the behest of the company in terms of the degree to which they were informed.

When the sales process was a linear one, it started at point one and finished at point four, and there were some very clear steps that the sales person and the customer would go through.

A single customer could often definitively express a single need. And we were taught as salespeople to ask them (through a series of funneled questions) to identify their need, before linking that need to a particular feature and benefit of our product or service. And that customer would often be able to make the decision, place the order, and use the product.

We were taught to pitch our product or solution and to do so relative to the competition or the next best alternative. We would often be equipped with sales aids and memo cards that listed out the relative features and benefits about our product versus the relative features and benefits of the next product.

But really, particularly with the amount of competition now available, it's very difficult to pitch your solution against the competition when the choice is so broad, and there is often such equity between the different products available.

Nowadays, there are multiple people involved, a variety of stakeholders, and many different decision-making points. It is not a one-dimensional approach anymore. It is far more project-based, and salespeople are project managing multiple projects and trying to influence many different people at any one time. They are professional change makers.

The fundamental change, now, is that it's not necessarily about the product, but what customers require in order to achieve longer-term goals and objectives, or to overcome problems or challenges which are often many and varied across the stakeholder base.

Being able to identify these problems and challenges up front and then engage in a credible, thought-provoking, discussion provides the salesperson with the ability to create a powerful dynamic for change.

IT'S NOT ABOUT THE PRODUCT

I see salespeople, not as product pushing, order taking, commodities, but as professional change makers and project managers, who have an inherent requirement to get people to think differently and consider what is possible.

That's right. *To consider what is possible.*

That's your job. My job. To get people to consider what is possible.

If the salesperson can think openly, creatively, and in terms of possibilities, then they have the opportunity to provoke the customer to think differently about their goals, objectives, problems, and challenges.

But it relies on the salesperson to actively create those opportunities and to take on the role of the professional change maker.

By creating an environment in which Critical Issues, ideas, and insights can be developed, salespeople will immediately start to create more value than ever before, and develop significance in the minds of customers.

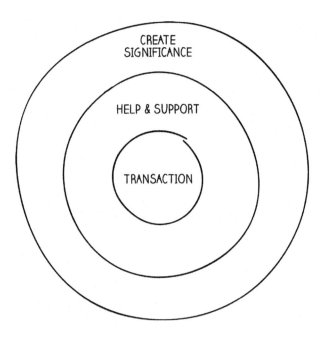

The old sales model was based on an approach where the transaction came first, which then led to the customer using the product, then receiving help and support, before eventually getting to a point where the salesperson was perhaps seen as valuable and significant.

We have to do everything we can to flip that model on its head.

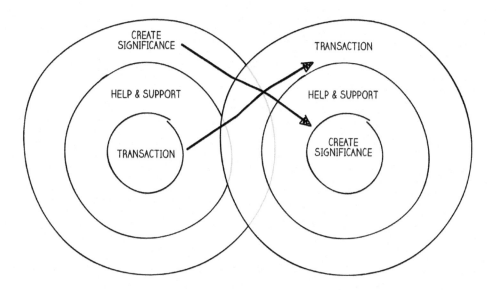

We need to focus on ways to create value and significance for customers first, to help and support them, so that finally the transaction or the sale follows as the consequence of the things that we do.

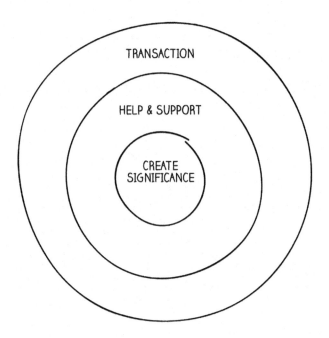

Far from being a vulnerable place to be, the salesperson must be the point of differentiation, because the product can't.

The product can't challenge and support the customer.

The product can't generate ideas, possibilities, or creativity.

The product can't provoke thought and discussion.

The product can't provide unique insights and perspectives.

And the product can't project manage a complex and multi-dimensional sale.

The only person who can do that is the salesperson.

Everything must be done to ensure the salesperson is equipped in the best possible way to be more effective than the next person, in order to create that value and significance for customers.

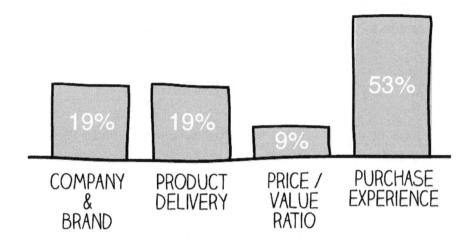

COMPANY & BRAND — 19%
PRODUCT DELIVERY — 19%
PRICE / VALUE RATIO — 9%
PURCHASE EXPERIENCE — 53%

Research by the Corporate Executive Board [5] showed that 53% of a customer's driver of loyalty for their choice of product (and their on-going use of it) was down to factors associated with what was described as 'the purchase experience'. That purchase experience included elements linked to a salesperson being able to offer unique and valuable perspectives that informed customers on issues affecting the market, and which helped them navigate alternatives and avoid potential mistakes, risks, and pitfalls. It included elements associated with the salesperson being easy to buy from, and being able to facilitate or connect customers with other like-minded stakeholders and peers.

What I want to explore, now, is the idea that those factors – those same factors associated with the purchase experience – can be broken down into three distinct types of activity that any salesperson can do. And the important thing about this is that these activities don't require anything else from the company.

They don't require the company to give them more stuff, or invest in any other way, or commit more resources. These are all things that an individual can do.

The three distinct areas are the salesperson's ability to *Teach*, their ability to *Coach*, and their ability to *Facilitate* or to connect.

TEACH, COACH, FACILITATE

Let's look at each of these in turn and explore them in a little more detail.

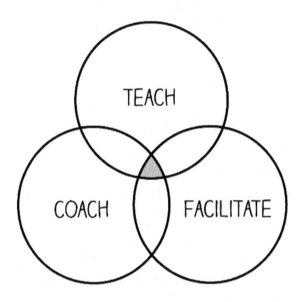

In terms of a salesperson's ability to Teach, I define that as the ability to impart expert knowledge.

I define a Coach as somebody who can indirectly help the other person to improve or to develop.

And I define Facilitate as the ability to directly help another person to achieve their objectives, often through connection with others.

To begin with, let's look at a non-commercial example and start outside anything too technical or commercial.

If I wanted to improve my performance in a specific sport, I could employ the services of a *Teacher*. A teacher could look at my current performance and instruct me in the three or four things that I need to do in order to improve, based on their expert knowledge.

I might work with a *Coach*, and that coach could look at my current performance, agree what future performance I wanted to achieve, and encourage me to try different things, to feel different things, and think of different things which would allow me to develop. So they wouldn't directly help me, but they would get me to try things and to think about things - to explore different ways of doing things, by increasing my awareness.

Finally, somebody could *Facilitate* my development, perhaps by connecting me with an elite person in that field who I could go and watch, and learn from. Or they might get me involved with a different group of individuals or a different club. Success is often a by-product of environment and the people we spend time with, so a facilitator might ensure that my environment was most appropriate for sporting success.

Now, let's bring this back to sales and a customer's point of view.

Over the course of our discussions, we've looked at how Critical Issues provide an opportunity to *Teach*. How exploring Current and Future States (provoking thought and discussion) offer the chance to *Coach*. And we've looked at how describing similar customers in similar positions not only Teaches but also provides the chance to *Facilitate*.

But that's only the beginning.

Here are some questions to reflect on and consider your role – to teach, coach, and facilitate.

Teach

- What are some of the possible ways in which you could teach your customers?
- What knowledge or insights might you possibly transfer?
- What expert knowledge do you have that you could share with your customers?
- Where might you identify issues or factors affecting their market?
- How might you possibly communicate with them on a regular basis?

Coach

- What are some of the possible ways you could take on the role of a coach with your customers?
- What questions might you ask which would allow you to explore their Current and Future States?
- How could you take steps to explore their goals, objectives, problems, or challenges?
- How might you help them consider alternative options?
- What could you do that would allow you to commit them to action?

Facilitate

- What are some of the possible ways in which you could take on the role of a facilitator?

- How might you connect customers with others who could help them achieve their goal or objective?

- How might you connect customers with others who might support or alleviate problems or challenges?

- Who do they admire, or see as a role model or centre of excellence, and how might you introduce them?

- What possible steps could you take that would give customers access to people, places, or resources that could help them?

In answering these questions and considering what we can do related to these three areas, we can identify the type of activity that is going to contribute to the greatest degree and have the biggest impact on a customer. If we can ensure that we focus on activity that is associated with the role of a teacher, a coach, and a facilitator, then that is high-value activity.

VALUE AND SIGNIFICANCE

This idea of generating 'value' is commonly viewed as a buzzword, and people are often heard saying that they 'create value' but without having any real clear understanding as to what that means.

Consider the different types of activity that might sit within each of these roles – teacher, coach, and facilitator. I want you to think about the different tasks that you could do, the different resources that you might require, different reasons to involve other people, and the types of other people that you could involve. I want you to consider how you might communicate with others and how you might get others buying. I want you to explore risks, consequences, challenges, assumptions, and barriers, and then I want you to consider what success might look like for the customer.

Just spend a few minutes, now, thinking about each of these areas - to Teach, to Coach, and to Facilitate. Try and get ten ideas in each of these buckets that allow you to think about ways in which you can create value for customers.

Teach	Coach	Facilitate
1	1	1
2	2	2
3	3	3
4	4	4
5	5	5
6	6	6
7	7	7
8	8	8
9	9	9
10	10	10

THE OLD DAYS ARE GONE

The salesperson as a teacher is somebody who can research issues that affect the customer. They can identify the issues that are most likely to impact the customer, and they can raise them in a way that is important, relevant, and objective, so as to demonstrate their credibility. These are Critical Issues.

The second step is for the salesperson to explore Current and Future States and provoke thought and discussion. By doing so, they take on the role of a coach, and for us, our definition of a salesperson as a coach is someone who helps a customer identify where they are today, and where they want to get to. Coaching helps them to see a picture of how they move from point A to point B.

Finally, the salesperson has to act as a facilitator. In other words, they facilitate the customer's thinking about what their current reality is, what their future reality might be, and the Gap that exists in how to solve it. The salesperson demonstrates how they've helped a similar customer in a similar position. And we do this using Experience Insights that are structured using the CASE model, which further demonstrates us as the Credible Expert.

And at the end of our process, we describe how our Unique Offering can help. This needs to be done at three levels: actual product level, the augmented product level, and then, finally, the core benefit.

So we know that the old days are gone. We know that success through a primary focus on product features, benefits, and solutions has gone, and that success now is reliant on creating more value and becoming more significant than the next person.

The idea that it's a risky strategy for a company to ensure that their salespeople are the point of differentiation is a huge error because it is only the salesperson now who can provide that point of differentiation.

We need to be clear on the link between value and significance. In creating value for customers, you become significant and when you're significant – you are valuable, If you are valuable, you create value.

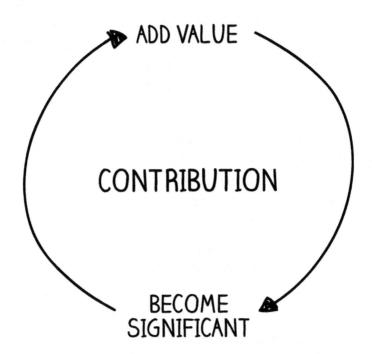

As with everything, *thinking* drives our activity and our results, and we should be thinking in terms of the three areas listed: the way that we Teach, the way that we Coach, and the way that we Facilitate. We should ensure that there is clear activity which sits in each of these areas, and we should do these things first, without expectation, and as often as possible.

The successful salesperson in the new economy is not the one who is fixed and rigid and who follows a script or a process, but the one who thinks in terms of possibilities, who can be flexible and creative, and who can project manage the sale and treat this as a multi-dimensional project (involving multiple stakeholders and multiple points).

The idea of value is far from a buzzword! This is something that is crucial and which we must create in order to succeed in the new selling economy.

KEY MESSAGES

- The only way to be successful in the new selling economy is to create value for our customers first

- As the Credible Expert, it is your role – your primary role – to find ways to create value for your customers

- We do this via three distinct areas, which are: to Teach, to Coach, and to Facilitate (connect).

- To teach is to transfer key knowledge or information which may be important, relevant, and credible, to the customer

- To coach is to help customers achieve their objective; and avoid mistakes, pitfalls, and errors

- To facilitate is to find ways to connect customers with like-minded peers or others in your network who can help facilitate their objective

- In doing the above, we create value, and this becomes a key part of our daily activity; as a result, the transaction or sale follows as a consequence

BRINGING IT ALL TOGETHER

Greater Possibilities. Increased Opportunities. A Better Way.

'WHAT'S IMPORTANT TO YOU?' IS NOW DEAD

Ten years ago, asking a customer (or potential customer) the question, 'what's important to you?' was perhaps the most commonly taught and often used question of the sales professional.

The origin and reason for that question was in the possible link that could be made between the unique features and benefits of the product (or service) and a customer need. At a time when technology was advancing at varying rates and with often wide-ranging differences between one product and the next, selecting a possible need and linking your point of differentiation to it seemed like the answer. And perhaps it was.

But now, when many providers can meet the needs of a customer, then in the absence of the sales professional provoking the thought of the customer, the customer will almost certainly default to either price or the product or service that they know. Clearly, if there's no discernible difference between the options available, one may as well choose the least expensive or most comfortable.

So that question is now redundant.

Because at a time when there is often little choice between the features and benefits of one product versus the next, at a point when the customer is as well-informed on the relative merits of Product A versus Product B as anyone, and when there is a multitude of choices available to them, asking 'what's important to you?' isn't going to provide the opportunity to differentiate yourself from the competition.

But this is still a contact sport.

And it's people who make the difference.

So the alternative lies in identifying themes of possible interest to the customer, researching those themes that are linked to relevant market and industry information related to your product or service, offering up those insights, relating this to the customer's world, and then linking to possible opportunities.

In reality, the change is from asking *'what's important to you?'* to identifying and raising *'what's important to you'* and then exploring and creating opportunities.

And it's not to say that a deep understanding of the product or service isn't critical – it is. It's just that in-depth product knowledge is table stakes.

What is likely to set you apart requires creativity, thinking in terms of possibilities, creating opportunities, and taking ownership of the business.

TEN BETTER WAYS

People provide the greatest opportunity for differentiation in the market

The changes that have occurred and are now evidently present in our selling world mean that it is the people – the salespeople – who are out there with customers daily, who now provide the single biggest point of differentiation. With so little to choose from between most of the top products, it is down to the salesperson to create maximum value and differentiation by provoking thought and discussion.

These changes require the salesperson to move away from the traditional, subservient, order-taking role to become the Credible Expert, who is seen as a peer. Someone who can provide important, relevant, and credible information, support the achievement of the customer's objectives, and facilitate connection with like-minded individuals and groups.

Involving others is crucial to achieving success

The role of Human Factors shows us that we don't operate in a vacuum but a complex system of interconnected components. These components are separated out into communication, decision-making, leadership, and situation awareness. And the salesperson who can gather information, identify the changes required, and adjust their behaviour will also be the one who can demonstrate acute self-awareness in the pursuit of stronger and more productive relationships.

But ultimately it requires us to involve others in the pursuit of our goals and objectives, open up to others, share with others, and think abundantly.

Those who consider greater possibilities create increased opportunities

In a world where salespeople are now project managers responsible for multiple projects, everyone becomes responsible for their own business. And in this environment, ideas are currency.

Ideas are the currency that converts into opportunities – for the individual, the team, the organisation, and the customer. And those who consider greater possibilities create increased opportunities. The individuals and teams who seek out and create the opportunities will be those who take on the ownership and the mindset of an Intrapreneur.

Ideas, creative thinking, and possibilities are the currency of our new selling environment, and it's those people who develop the mindset of an owner who cultivate ideas in abundance.

Our focus determines our results

The days of meeting with the individual who is the butcher, the baker, and the candlestick-maker, are gone. Rather, we now work and operate within a complex network of interconnected individuals and groups, and identifying the right people to spend our time with is a key success factor.

To do so, we need to objectify the subjective with a view to improving our return on investment. The ability to acknowledge that there are variations in the power, interest, and influence that individuals hold in the context of the future achievement of our commercial objective is followed by the need to manage those people differently. How and where we choose to spend our time, and the quantity, quality, and direction of our activity, will inevitably determine our outcome.

Segmenting customers and establishing 'groups' helps to answer the question, 'where *could* I spend my time?' It is the first step towards improving the efficiency of sales activity.

Targeting allows you to make an informed decision about where to spend your time and how to increase your return on investment, and is the next step in improving personal efficiency. It answers the question, 'where *will* I spend my time?'

The clarity, uniqueness, and purpose of our message ensures that customers become advocates

Within the stakeholder map, we have the opportunity to turn our customers into advocates. Many of them will be required to re-sell and re-articulate why someone should work with us. And the simple fact of the matter is that if we aren't clear on the answers to those questions, there is no way we can expect our customers to be.

Being clear on what you specifically do, how you're different to the competition, and why someone should work with you, are the fundamental questions to answer. The answers, though, as simple as they may ultimately be, are not necessarily easy to arrive at. And so the Intrapreneur, the Credible Expert, is required not just to consider them but to revise and practice them until the message is a compelling one.

People prefer to receive information in different ways. Understanding those preferences allows the message to be adapted for maximum impact. It avoids the risk of 'one size fits all', or delivering information that is perceived as irrelevant. In essence, it considers the 'niche of one', otherwise known as 'ultra-targeting'.

We frame our offer from our customer's perspective

By framing our offer from the customer's perspective, we have the opportunity to drive the customer journey and the customer conversation. Rather than asking, 'what's important to you' we have to describe 'what's important to you', ensuring that the

Critical Issue is important, relevant, and objective. Whether the issues are representative of macro, strategic or micro challenges, the approach requires planning, preparation, and practice.

With this in mind, it is no longer right to expect salespeople to lurch from one call to the next, trying to complete a fixed number of calls per day, per week. Rather, it's more appropriate to enable the sales team that does the work – the hard work – to become Credible Experts.

Critical Issues demonstrate to the customer that, in addition to knowing about our product or service, we can create value and significance because we understand the customer's world and the issues which matter. It provides the opportunity for us to be seen as Credible Experts in our field, and a valuable resource when time is scarce.

Provoking thought creates a powerful dynamic for change

The days of the subservient, transactional, order-taker are gone. Customers need, want, and expect their salespeople to be able to provoke thought and discussion. For as much as we should leave our customer meetings considering whether the time that we spent will deliver a positive return on investment, our customers should also be doing the same.

Provoking thought and discussion, and having customers consider the Gap that exists between where they are today and where they might be, creates a powerful dynamic for change. And with it comes the clarity about whether productivity, performance, profile, or purse is the key driver of customer change.

Customers need to visualise what a buying future with you as a supplier may look like. They need to explore what a positive and constructive future could be like, and balance that against their current reality. Whilst the Critical Issue provides context and a platform for the discussion, it is the sales person's ability to explore challenges and hopes that helps the customer create a future vision.

Highlighting the Gap between the customer's Current and Future State by exploring their challenges and hopes creates a tension between the world they currently occupy and the one they might aspire to. It allows the salesperson to position themselves, not simply as the product or service specialist, but as the facilitator of that enhanced future.

The stories we tell transform what a customer believes is possible

Customers often find it difficult to see what a future buying vision may look like. By highlighting Experience Insights, salespeople are able to support that vision in a non-adversarial manner.

Customers want certainty; they want to know that you've helped other people in a similar position, and they want to know that they are dealing with a credible expert. Furthermore, many of the broader and senior stakeholders we are now required to spend time with do not care about the intricate details of the product or the service.

They want to know what it delivers, how it links to their key driver of change, and how it alleviates the pressure created as a result of their Critical Issue. And we do this through the vehicle of story, where we helped a similar customer in a similar position.

Our offer becomes compelling when we create the desire for change

It is essential for the salesperson to demonstrate their Unique Offering. It requires them to present the product or service not only at the foundational level of its key characteristics, but also to demonstrate the augmented service and core benefits of any future working relationship. At the heart of the core benefit is the reason why a customer should buy the product or service, and links to the Gap and the Critical Issue.

By considering the offering at the three levels – the actual, augmented, and core benefit – it allows the salesperson the chance to link the product or service back through to the customer's Critical Issue and the Gap that exists between their Current and Future States.

Our results are directly proportional to the value we create for our customers

Far from being a buzzword, or a nice-feeling, or approach, creating value for customers is now the only way to ensure continued and sustained success. It requires the salesperson to look for ways to create value linked to their role as a Teacher, Coach, and Facilitator (TCF) and demonstrate their worth as such.

Whilst to teach is to transfer key knowledge and insights, the coach is to help customers achieve their objectives, facilitation is about connections with like-minded individuals or groups. We teach by highlighting Critical Issues, coach by provoking thought and discussion about Current and Future States, and facilitate by connecting customers with others who can support the achievement of their objectives.

THE FINAL CHAPTER

The ideas here are simple ones.

The thesis of this book is that, once you have acknowledged the importance of your role in the new changed selling economy – which includes how you think, how you act and how you interact – you select the right customers, you research and identify Critical Issues, use those to frame a thought-provoking discussion around current and future states, and demonstrate how you've helped similar customers in similar positions, before accurately articulating in a compelling way how your offer can support them. All the while you're building tension in the sales journey so as to create desire for your offer, whilst creating value and significance.

There we are.

36,000 words distilled down into just 103 words.

Maybe I should have just written these 103 and published them online. That would have saved some time, effort, and money.

But then again, there's significant difference between simple and easy.

Simple is acknowledging that the world has changed and that it's the salesperson who offers the single biggest point of differentiation.

Simple is knowing that Human Factors play a significance role in the way we interact within the system we work in; and that communication, decision making, leadership, and situational awareness underpin that system.

Simple is accepting that it's your thinking which determines your activity that determines your results.

Simple is acknowledging the need to deliver a three-part Engage Statement to clearly and concisely articulate what you do, how you're different to the competition, and why someone should work with you.

Simple is describing the requirement to map stakeholders against power, interest, and influence, in order to consider where to spend your time.

Simple is understanding the need to identify Critical Issues which are important, relevant, and objective and that are visible in macro, strategic, or micro areas.

Simple is describing the four types of questions to explore current and future states, to consider where customers are today versus where they might be in the future.

Simple is acknowledging that there are four key drivers of change and describing a time when you've helped a similar customer in a similar position.

Simple is understanding the need to present your Unique Offering at three levels – the actual product, the augmented product, and the core product.

Simple is seeing the role of the salesperson as a Teacher, Coach, and Facilitator.

Simple is knowing that greater possibilities lead to increased opportunities and a better way.

All of these ideas are simple.

But there's a fundamental difference between simple and easy.

Not everything can be distilled down into a pithy maxim or 140 character message, and a dummies guide fails to acknowledge the hard work – mental and emotional – required to succeed in business in the new world in which we live and work.

In my first book, I closed by saying:

'…Life is a contact sport, business is a contact sport and ultimately it is people and the way in which we interact with people that will make the difference. That is what we need to focus on and to remove the learned behaviours that are inhibiting our growth, development and greater success.'

That still stands true today and is likely to be a consistent truth for many years to come. It is the way in which you interact with people that will make the difference.

What I hope you've taken over the course of this book are some key ideas, concepts, and frameworks that, when applied, will make a difference to you and your business. I hope that you take one thing – even if only one – that you can apply for the betterment of what you're working towards.

There is now a sizeable opportunity available for anyone who is willing to do the hard work required, to position themselves as the Credible Expert. History will look back on this time and acknowledge that the tide turned – that it wasn't the product or service that made the greatest difference, but the people and the roles they played every day with their customers.

Make sure that, when you look back on your career, you can say that you took that opportunity; that you made the most of the changing dynamics of the world we sold into, and that you positioned yourself as the Credible Expert.

TO POSITION YOURSELF AS THE CREDIBLE EXPERT

Acknowledge the importance of how you think, act, and interact, to
Select The Right Customers
Deliver Compelling Messages
Identify Critical Issues
Provoke Thought And Discussion
Highlight Experience Insights
Demonstrate Your Unique Offering
Create Value And Significance

TO FIND A BETTER WAY, KNOW THAT

People provide the greatest opportunity for differentiation in the
market
Involving others is crucial to achieving success
Those who consider greater possibilities create increased opportunities
Our focus determines our results
The clarity, uniqueness, and purpose of our message ensures that
customers become advocates
We frame our offer from our customer's perspective
Provoking thought creates a powerful dynamic for change
The stories we tell transform what a customer believes is possible
Our offer becomes compelling when we create the desire for change
Our results are directly proportional to the value we create for our
customers

REFERENCES

1-4   Bolton P, Historical Statistics, SN/SG/4252, House of Commons Library, 27th November 2012

5   Adamson, Dixon, Toman, The End Of Solution Sales, Harvard Business Review, July-August 2012

6   http://chfg.org/tag/martin-bromiley/ accessed 19th September 2016

7-8   http://www.forbes.com/sites/keldjensen/2012/04/12/intelligence-is-overrated-what-you-really-need-to-succeed/#66b1e8f46375 accessed 19th September 2016

9   Andy Gilbert, The Art Of Making A Difference, A Powerful Guide To Achieving Personal And Business Success, Published 1st June 2015, Andy Gilbert

10   Timothy Gallway, The Inner Game of Tennis: The ultimate guide to the mental side of peak performance, 18th June 2015, Main Market

11   Freeman et al, The Journal of Neuroscience, August 6, 2014, 34(32): 10573–10581

12   Van Vliet, V. (2012). Communication Model by Albert Mehrabian. Accessed 19th September 2016 from http://www.toolshero.com/communication-management/communication-model-mehrabian/

13   Lord Carter Report, 1st February 2016, accessed 19th September 2016 from https://www.gov.uk/government/uploads/system/uploads/attachment_data/file/499229/Operational_productivity_A.pdf

14   http://www.huffingtonpost.co.uk/entry/nhs-funding_uk_57d512a3e4b0d45ff87210db accessed 19th September 2016

15   https://www.parliament.uk/business/publications/research/key-issues-parliament-2015/social-change/ageing-population/ accessed 19th September 2016

16   Michael David Harris, Insight Selling: How to sell value and differentiate your product with insight scenarios, 6th January 2014, Sales and Marketing Press

17   Everett Rogers, Diffusion Of Innovators, 5th Edition, 17th November 2003, Free Press

18   https://www.thinkwithgoogle.com/interviews/winning-the-zero-moment-of-truth-b2b.html accessed 19th September 2016

Lightning Source UK Ltd.
Milton Keynes UK
UKOW05f1332141116

287621UK00011B/679/P

9 781911 121206